Jackie
God wants to set you free
and we will do this
together. There is nothing
he wouldn't do to save you.
If He did it for me He will &
can do it for you. If you believe
He will do it. Take it one day at
a time. If He can save me
He will save you. Get ready for
God to Rock your world!

atthetablehm.net

WHEN GODLY PEOPLE DO UNGODLY THINGS

WHEN GODLY PEOPLE DO UNGODLY THINGS

ARMING YOURSELF *in the* AGE OF SEDUCTION

BETH MOORE

PUBLISHING GROUP

NASHVILLE, TENNESSEE

ISBN: 978-0-8054-2465-2

Published by B&H Publishing Group,
Nashville, Tennessee

Subject Heading: CHRISTIAN LIVING

nless otherwise stated all Scripture citations are from the NIV
the Holy Bible, New International Version, copyright © 1973,
1978, 1984 by International Bible Society; other versions cited
e NASB, the New American Standard Bible, © the Lockman
oundation, 1960, 1962, 1963, 1968, 1971, 1972, 1973, 1975,
1977; used by permission; AMP, The Amplified Bible, Old
estament copyright © 1962, 1964 by Zondervan Publishing
House, used by permission, and the New Testament © The
Lockman Foundation 1954, 1958, used by permission; KJV, the
King James Version.

10 11 12 13 14 15   10 09 08 07

To L. L.

You have been an unspeakable inspiration—
especially at times when I've grieved while a few others
refused to go the distance and let their Redeemer redeem.
What needless defeat!
I am so proud of you. Can you imagine how He must feel?
A great harvest awaits you, Dear One.
I can't wait to look over your shoulder and celebrate!

ACKNOWLEDGMENTS

Though many have supported this message and helped bring it from heart to page, One must be acknowledged over all others. My Father, I will never understand the extravagant nature of Your grace and mercy. You continue to take the worst blights on my Christian track record and use them for good. If anyone has tested Romans 8:28, surely I did! I am proof You are true to Your Word. My Lord and my God, the Love of my life, thank You so much for not being ashamed of me. I will proclaim Your loving-kindness as long as I live. I adore You.

Keith, Amanda, and Melissa, what would I do if you were too embarrassed or private to allow me the freedom to use my own testimonies, failures, and experiences publicly? I love the three of you so much. Keith, you are my best friend. Thank you for also believing so strongly in this message of warning, protection, and full redemption. Girls, I can't leave you a perfect track record for an inheritance but in the words of Peter in Acts 3:6, "such as I have give I thee." Lessons learned. Grace received. Love lavished. These are the things of your inheritance. Pour them out in humility and abundance upon others.

Susan and Sabrina, thank you for not resting until this message got out. I will never forget how you reacted when Satan hit me with second thoughts. Your experiences and testimonies were inexpressible inspiration throughout these pages. I love all of you at Living Proof Ministries so much. Let's watch our backs, Ladies! Satan's going to be mad.

My brothers and sisters at Broadman & Holman, I am so grateful for your partnership in this work. I have never felt more strongly about a message God has given me. Having a publisher who did not believe in the full restoration of the repentant would be a laughable irony in my case. I wouldn't be in ministry if God were not a willing and able Redeemer. Thank you for not being afraid of this message and for leaving so "in tact." We said it loud. Now, may God make it clear!

Finally, I am so grateful to God for those He appointed to risk telling me their stories. None of them had any idea so many others were experiencing similar horrors. May God expose the enemy of our souls, and may the Body of Christ become equipped in this unparalleled age of seduction. The time is now.

CONTENTS

PREFACE

his book represents one of the most unique writing experiences I've ever had with God. Unbeknownst to me, He's been writing each chapter on my heart for several years. When the message for this book was complete (in His estimation—*not mine!*), God compelled me to ink it on paper with a force of the Holy Spirit unparalleled in my experience. He whisked me to the mountains of Wyoming where I entered solitary confinement with Him, and in only a few short weeks, I wrote the last line. My most overwhelming emotion at this point is *relief.* My soul is at rest. I have done to the best of my understanding what God seemed to require of me with a relentless passion.

On behalf of all authors who seek the sole leadership of the Holy Spirit, please allow me to say that we don't just pick and choose our subject matter. In fact, sometimes God assigns us a message that is more radical than we'd choose to be and requires more transparency than we'd ever want to invite! I am being as honest as I know how to be when I say that I did not write these pages by simple preference. I wrote them because had I not, the rocks in my yard would have cried out. What God does with what He's required is His business. I entrust this message entirely to the One who delivered it while I sat bug-eyed.

Certainly I'm not audaciously implying that this book is written under the same kind of divine inspiration as the Holy

Scriptures! The Word of God is our only volume of pure truth. We mortals no doubt taint everything we touch however accidentally. What I'm saying is that I wrote this message to the best of my ability under the guidance of the Holy Spirit, and I do not believe it conceptually departs from the precepts of God's Word. I may unknowingly err in interpretation or application, but the overall message of warning, redemption, and restoration are consistent with a God so merciful and courageous, He would dare use a pauper like me.

The only other of my manuscripts Satan tried as hard to hinder or destroy was *Breaking Free*. He hates to let go of a captive. He also hates being exposed as the fraud he is and *that's* one of the chief goals of this book. My specific prayer for this message is threefold:

- that God will use the pages of this book to shed light on Satan's massive campaign, in our current and future generations, to seduce the saints.
- that God will use this message to remind a battered and bruised believer how loved he is and how much the Father longs for his complete restoration. We have never gone so far that we can't come home. *Oh, thank You, Lord!*
- that many readers will wise up to Satan's seductive schemes and fortify their lives *before* he traps them into something ungodly.

This book is written in three parts. Part 1 is the warning, both biblical and experiential, that Satan is heightening his attack on devout believers in Jesus Christ. Part 2 comprises ways we can fortify ourselves against Satan's full-scale attack on the lives of the elect in the latter days. Part 3 is the road home for the one who has been deceived and seduced by the enemy into a season of ungodliness. If you are fairly convinced you are a victim of satanic seduction, please read the book in this important order: Part 1, Part 3, then Part 2. All others should read the message in the order it is written.

When Godly People Do Ungodly Things would never have been written without the vigilant prayer and fasting of a thousand prayer warriors who built a firewall fortress around me for several weeks. I am unspeakably humbled by their around-the-clock provision of prayer protection. Many took "hits" on my behalf that can only be explained as spiritual warfare. I am astonished and deeply indebted to them for their willingness to war so faithfully on behalf of this message. They enabled me to write while entirely alone many miles from home without experiencing a single hint of oppression. Satan was utterly defeated.

One of the peculiarities about this assignment is that God also required me to fast. He would not release me to eat until the very end of each day after all writing for that day was accomplished. Sometimes He would not release me until the end of the next day. Never before has He asked me to do such a thing while writing a book. Many authors may fast in advance of a project but we feel we need the *brain food* during the actual process. This time God would not permit any such approach. To tell you how adamant He was, the one time I thought I'd be fine to eat breakfast; my thoughts became completely warbled and confused until midafternoon. The requirements of this message were so unusual and intriguing to me that I couldn't help wondering why. Finally

God gave me understanding and I realized that He was applying the principle Christ introduced in Mark 9:29 (KJV). This book—written specifically to expose one of the most insidious assaults of the evil one—would *"come forth by nothing, but by prayer and fasting."* What God required of a thousand prayer warriors and me gave us just a hint how much the enemy was raging against us in the heavenlies.

Once again I find my insecure self wanting to issue some kind of disclaimer about my mental and spiritual health. I really am a pretty normal person. *I think.* I can tease with the best of them and can take a joke. *If it's funny.* I am a regular wife and mom. (And does anyone happen to remember that one of the last books I wrote was a sweet, inoffensive mommy book?) I love dogs and I really like chocolate malts. I am a maniac for Mexican food. I like long Sunday afternoon naps and digging in my flowerbed. Some of my neighbors don't even run in the house when I'm out in the front yard. I'm just your average girl, for heaven's sake!

I didn't ask to write some of the kinds of messages God has appointed me. Believe me, some of the works God has assigned me have not been without sacrifice. My mother went to her grave wondering why I couldn't "just be funny" like I "used to be." Although I certainly received her love, I never received her blessing for the turn my ministry took toward freedom for the captives. Choosing God's approval over hers was a monumental test for me. She's not the only one who liked me better when I did everything far safer. Some of my deeply loved fellow Baptists probably wonder from time to time why I have to be so edgy while brothers and sisters at the other end of the spectrum just wish I'd go ahead and jump off the edge with them. I'm not going to. I cannot write to please man as much as I'd like to at times. So, when you've turned the last page, if you're not *pleased,* kindly consider telling God and not me. My self-esteem is shakier than His.

Lastly, I want you to know how honored I am to serve you no matter who you are or where you've been. You are a lavishly loved child of God. I humble myself before you and even now have come to my knees in your behalf where I'd like to pray for you.

> *Father, I am so grateful for the opportunity to serve this brother or sister in the faith. I readily and willingly esteem Your child as better than myself. I do not wish to lord authority over a single one. I wish to serve at the feet of any who will allow me the privilege. How I pray that Your words will fall powerfully upon this child and that mine will be forgotten. I echo the petition I've prayed throughout this journey that You would not let me lead a single one in error. If I have unknowingly left something in this manuscript that is not of You, I beg Your forgiveness, and I pray his or her mind will not absorb it. I pray that You will give Your child ears to hear, eyes to see, and a mind to conceive every word of Yours in this message. Help my brother or sister to approach these concepts with transparency before You. Even if he or she is reading this book in someone else's behalf, I pray each reader will hear You speak straight to his own heart. In Jesus' name I bind the attempt of the enemy to cause any desperate reader to grow an attachment*

to me rather than You. You are our only salvation.
God forbid that any flesh glory in Your presence. You
are the only One worthy of a second thought.

You are the love of my life, Jesus. I want others to
love You with absolute abandon. Steal our hearts,
Lord Jesus, and consume our minds with Your truth.
We are otherwise dreadfully at risk of seduction.
Expose your child's vicious enemy and any ground he
or she has unknowingly surrendered to him. Rise to
Your feet and fight on behalf of Your beloved child,
Mighty Warrior. Redeem every single hit and every
single hurt caused by the enemy of souls. Cause each
precious reader to see this journey to its completion.
You will be faithful to finish what You start in each
one. I thank You in advance that none who allow
Your Word to abide will ever be unchanged. In the
powerful, life-giving name of my Deliverer and
Redeemer, Jesus, Amen.

PART I

THE
WARNING

———

PRIME TARGETS

I am terrified . . ." Not just a tad concerned. Terrified. I'm convinced that's what the apostle Paul meant when he wrote, "I
am afraid that just as Eve was deceived by the serpent's cunning,
your minds may somehow be led astray from your sincere and
pure devotion to Christ" (2 Cor. 11:3).

For a people who fear so much that is unnecessary, we have
doused the term *afraid* with our bottled water until it slips com-
fortably into sentences such as, "I'm afraid the ball game might
be rained out." That's not what the fiery apostle meant.

The Greek verb *phobeo* encompasses a far greater alarm than
tempered concern. Imagine the pitch of Paul's voice erupting
from the passion he felt for the infant church in Corinth. I think
he was terrified for them. Mind you, he wasn't afraid of the serpent. He preached alertness and aggressive resistance, never
phobia. He was terrified that this inexperienced and passionate
young church might fall for the serpent's schemes.

I will probably live my whole life without grasping a fraction of
Paul's spiritual perspective, but I have come to share a heaping cupful of his prophetic alarm in this unsettling Scripture. *I am terrified.*

A strange thing began to happen soon after my books, *Breaking Free* and *Praying God's Word,* were released. Probably because I admit to such a flawed and sinful past, letters began stacking on my desk from Christians confessing, often for the very first time, to harrowing rounds of defeat at the hands of the devil.

You may be thinking, *So what else is new? Satan has attacked man since his creation.*

I'd like to suggest that there *is* something about this spiritual phenomenon that might just have taken demonic assault to a whole "new" level. In the course of this ministry I've read countless letters, and I have come to discern the difference between blatant accounts of mercifully forgiven rebellion and the testimonials I'm talking about here.

What has terrified me is the growing stack of letters from believers who loved God and walked with Him faithfully for years then found themselves suddenly overtaken by a tidal wave of temptation and unholy assault.

Many believers are convinced such things can't happen. "Not to *good* Christians." They are wrong. And through the course of this book, I hope to prove it.

Skeptics ask, "How do you know these people are not lying or trying to make themselves sound like innocent victims?" Undoubtedly because I was so desperate and prayerful for discernment, through the last several years God has developed such an acute awareness in my spirit toward deception that the ability makes me uncomfortable.

I don't quite know how to explain it, but the Holy Spirit in me often causes me to detect when something is not what it seems. I am convinced many of these accounts of formerly pure lives suddenly knee-deep in the mire are absolutely authentic. Not one of them presents him or herself as an innocent victim. They are horrified and taken aback at what they have done and appear capable of doing. A flood of shame pours forth like rusty water from a busted pipe. (That's one way you can detect who's at the bottom of it. Shame is Satan's game.) Shockingly few of those who have told me their stories were looking for excuses. They were looking for explanations. Big difference.

Another skeptic might ask, "How do you know they are telling you the whole story?" I don't doubt they may not be telling me the whole story. I'm not sure they *know* the whole story. I surely don't know mine. I'll have questions about some of the things that have happened to me until I die!

One of the chief purposes of this book is to hopefully shed a little light on parts of our stories that we *don't* know but, thankfully, *can* know. Over and over I've heard renditions of the following statement: "For the life of me, I can't figure out how something like this could have happened." When we turn the last page of this book, we still won't know everything about how godly people can turn around and do ungodly things, but I pray we'll know more than we do this moment.

My insatiable search for all the answers nearly kept me from writing this book. There are still plenty of things I don't fully understand, and I will openly admit to them as we reach those places.

I am fairly convinced that some of the pieces are simply hidden from our eyes and we won't have crystal-clear understanding this side of heaven. The apostle Paul himself taught that the spirit of lawlessness has a *secret power* (2 Thess. 2:7). As much as I wanted to wait to finish this book until I understood it all, God placed such an urgency in my spirit that I could not delay another second. I am too terrified for the Body of Christ.

I need to clearly state that three streams of evidence lead me to my conclusions in this book. As we proceed, I want to ask you to consider the significance of each.

I've told you the first stream of evidence: the testimonies of scores of believers. Now let's turn to the second. I don't care how many testimonials I received, I would not give what they suggest—that godly people *can* suddenly do ungodly things—a second thought except that Scripture completely supports the idea. Take a good look in the Amplified Bible at the Scripture I quoted at the beginning of this chapter, including the verse that precedes it.

> For I am zealous for you with a godly eagerness and a divine jealousy, for I have betrothed you to one Husband, to present you a chaste virgin to Christ. But [now] I am fearful, lest that even as the serpent beguiled Eve by his cunning, so your minds may be corrupted and seduced from wholehearted and sincere and pure devotion to Christ. (2 Cor. 11:2–3 AMP)

Wholehearted. Sincere. Pure devotion to Christ. To you, what kind of person does the apostle Paul seem to be describing? That very kind of person can be beguiled by the enemy, whose utmost fantasy is to corrupt and seduce the real thing. Unsettling, isn't it?

Let's take a look at another unnerving statement. In Galatians 6:1, the apostle Paul wrote:

> Brethren, if any person is overtaken in misconduct or sin of any sort, you who are spiritual—who are responsive to and controlled by the Spirit—should set him right and restore and reinstate him, without any sense of superiority and with all gentleness, keeping an attentive eye on yourself, lest you should be tempted also. (AMP)

Even the one who is spiritual, "responsive to and controlled by the Spirit," can be tempted by the same sins that have overtaken another. One might argue, "Yes, the one who is spiritual might be tempted, but he surely wouldn't fall for it." Ah, I believe I hear the familiar echo of 1 Corinthians 10:12 in mine ear: "Therefore let any one who thinks he stands—who feels sure that he has a steadfast mind and is standing firm—take heed lest he fall [into sin]" (AMP).

Not only *can* the godly suddenly sprawl into a ditch from a solid, upright path, I believe many do. I am convinced, as the days, weeks, and months blow off the Kingdom calendar, that the casualties are growing in number by harrowing leaps and bounds. Many just aren't talking because they are scared half to death. Not so much of God as they are of the church. To say that the Body of Christ would be shocked to know how bloody and bruised by defeat we are is a gross understatement. Among the better pieces of news is that God is most assuredly not shocked. Grieved perhaps, but not shocked. You see, He told us this was coming.

I told you three streams of evidence have led me to the conclusions in this book. The first was the testimony of believers who have been seduced into sin. The second is the warning in Scripture that Spirit-filled believers can be overtaken. The third stream of evidence has to do with the end of the age.

In Christ's discourse to His disciples concerning the signs of His coming and the end of the age, He emphatically warned them of an increase in deception, in lawlessness, and in wickedness. Undoubtedly the New Testament supports an ever increasing wickedness that will rise in furious temperature until "the lawless one will be revealed, whom the Lord Jesus will overthrow with the breath of his mouth and destroy by the splendor of his coming" (2 Thess. 2:8). If the apostle Paul could testify in his generation that "the secret power of lawlessness is already at work" (2 Thess. 2:7), who can begin to estimate the acceleration that has taken place over the last one hundred years?

The biblical study called *eschatology* deals with the "ultimate" or "last things." Different scholars of wholehearted commitment to Christ disagree over many details of eschatology. Some scholars believe that we either have entered or are about to enter the time of escalating conflict that will usher in the return of Christ—the last days. Other scholars point to evidence that the biblical last days extend from the time of the apostles to the return of Christ. Either way, beloved, we are living in the time closer than ever before to the end events of Christian history.

Jesus warned His followers of a time of severe persecution, a time of "great distress, unequaled from the beginning of the world until now" (Matt. 24:21). He warned, "Then you will be handed over to be persecuted and put to death, and you will be hated by all nations because of me. At that time many will turn away from the faith and will betray and hate each other, and many false prophets will appear and deceive many people. Because of the increase of wickedness, the love of most will grow cold" (Matt. 24:9–12). These warnings of Christ have applied to all ages, but many Bible scholars believe they point specifically to the war going on in our present and near future.

Combined with the evidence of stream one and stream two, I'm convinced we must prepare ourselves to deal with the assault that is here and the one that is coming.

Thank goodness, the news is not all bad. Christ also prophesied that the "gospel of the kingdom will be preached in the whole world as a testimony to all nations" (Matt. 24:14). The president of the International Mission Board in Richmond, Virginia, told me that they are seeing record numbers of people surrendering to foreign missions and can explain it in no other way than the pending fulfillment of prophecy. Furthermore, Scripture prophesies an unprecedented outpouring of the Holy Spirit on God's sons and daughters in the latter days. I have very little doubt that favorable prophecies like these are some of the very works Satan is trying his hardest to both undermine and delay by attacking servants of God.

Clearly, we are living in the best of days and the worst of days. While fresh winds of the Spirit are blowing upon many of our churches and a double portion of anointing is bestowed on many believers, the Word also strongly suggests that we are occupying planet Earth during the scariest time in human history to date. You only need look as far as your own community to stare 2 Timothy 3:1–5 in the face.

But mark this: There will be terrible times in
the last days. People will be lovers of themselves,
lovers of money, boastful, proud, abusive, dis-
obedient to their parents, ungrateful, unholy, without love, unforgiving, slanderous, without
self-control, brutal, not lovers of the good, treach-
erous, rash, conceited, lovers of pleasure rather
than lovers of God—having a form of godliness
but denying its power. (2 Tim. 3:1–5)

Take a good look at the words "without love." The King James
Version captures the meaning of the original Greek with the phrase
"without natural affection." The word *astorgos* means "without
family love."[1] Surely no previous society has ever matched the escalating percentages of crimes within the family unit. I believe no former generation has held such staggering statistics of parents killing
their own children and children killing their own parents.

Perhaps the end of this age is best characterized biblically by
the word *escalation*. Christ compared the signs of the end of our
present age to birth pains (Matt. 24:8)—an analogy many of us
who have given birth understand with startling clarity. With
time, the pains grow far more intense and much closer together.
I am not remotely an expert in biblical eschatology, but the birth
pains for a coming era have vastly increased and intensified, particularly in the last fifty years.

Many argue that every generation of believers since the ascen-
sion of Christ has believed itself to be in the last days. While that
could be true, no former generation has possessed our satellite
and Internet capabilities, which pave the way for a worldwide

"hookup." No previous generation could boast the astonishing modes of worldwide travel and research capabilities that ours can. The twentieth century trotted its way onto the Kingdom calendar by horse and buggy, then pushed the speed of light as it waved its way out through cyberspace.

If we have indeed entered the last days, which I believe we have, we still have no way of knowing how long they may last. While date setting is a waste of time, learning how to cope with escalating crisis is not.

Our present purpose is not to study the mounting statistics of fulfilled prophecy. We want to understand how godly people can do ungodly things and to search out biblical remedies.

So what does the approach of the end have to do with godly people falling before a satanic assault? Everything! Revelation 12 tells us that the "ancient serpent called the devil" is "filled with fury, because he knows that his time is short" (Rev. 12:9, 12).

If you and I have reason to be interested in end-time events, imagine what is at stake for Satan! Believe me, he knows every single sign of the end, and he reads them with the panic of one reading his own obituary in advance. The closer the calendar draws to Christ's return and the devil's crushing defeat, the more furious he becomes.

Who are the chief targets of Satan's ever increasing fury? *We are.* Why? I believe Satan has two primary motivations: (1) to exact revenge on God by wreaking havoc on His children and (2) to try to incapacitate the believer's God-given ability to overcome him.

Revelation 12:11 says, "They overcame him by the blood of the Lamb and by the word of their testimony." Once we are covered by the blood of the Lamb, like the angel of death during the first Passover night, Satan cannot enter our abode. Those of us who have received Christ as our personal Savior are the dwelling places of the Holy Spirit (1 Cor. 6:19–20). Our doorposts are covered by the precious blood of our Passover Lamb. Neither Satan nor his demons can enter us.

The more we understand what the covering of Christ's blood means to us, the more we overcome a foe that is otherwise far too strong for us. Satan's worst nightmare is being overcome—particularly by measly mortals. He knows the Bible says we overcome our accuser in two primary ways. If he can do nothing about the blood of the Lamb covering the redeemed, what's a devil to do? Go for the word of their testimony! Satan is out to destroy the testimony of the believer in Christ. The more influential the testimony, the better. His murderous eye is on the sparrow, and he doesn't have much time. His strategy is to kill as many birds as possible with one stone.

We don't have to be rocket scientists to figure out that Satan's favorite prey is a person of godly influence. Peter spoke from the vantage point of personal experience when he said, "Your enemy the devil prowls around like a roaring lion looking for someone to devour" (1 Pet. 5:8). Satan had nearly eaten him alive. Peter continued, "Resist him, standing firm in the faith, because you know that your brothers throughout the world are undergoing the same kind of sufferings" (v. 9).

Allow me to jump ahead to subject matter we'll approach further in our study by saying that we are certainly not sitting ducks. Later in part 1, we'll learn why some godly people are more vulnerable than others. Then in part 2, we'll learn ways to guard ourselves against that kind of vulnerability.

For now I want you to take a look back at the final word in the Scripture I last quoted from 1 Peter 5:9. The word is *sufferings*. I don't know how many times I've repeated the statement I'm about to make, but I'll keep saying it until at least one skeptic hears: *Not everyone in a stronghold of sin is having a good time.*

Many people who by the grace of God have never been "had" by the devil wrongly assume that all departures from godliness are nothing but defiance, rebellion, and proofs of inauthenticity. They have no idea of the suffering involved when someone with a genuine heart for God slips from the path.

Tangling with a roaring lion who is trying his hardest to devour you can constitute real and authentic suffering. In fact, I have suffered more at the flesh-ripping paws of the raging lion than anything else.

I lived a measure of my young life in rebellion and in defeat, but I can say without hesitation that the times the enemy came after me most ferociously were *not* those times. During times of rebellion, all the devil had to do was cheer me on and tell me to keep up the good work.

The times in my life when I believe the powers of darkness raged most violently against me were seasons when I had never loved God more. I was not walking in sin previous to either of the times I fought my hardest battles with the kingdom of darkness.

At first I thought I was the exception. I can well remember my devastating failure in my college years. I thought I was the only young woman in the whole Christian world who ever fell grievously into sin after sincerely devoting her life to vocational ministry. I was completely devastated. Totally shamed. I had no idea where to turn. With no outside help or a single explanation for what I had experienced, I did my best to pull it together.

Satan waited until I had accrued a much better track record, had grown a little more confident in a consistent walk, and looked suspiciously like God could make me slightly dangerous . . . then he hit me again. *Hard*. This time God said, "Have you had about enough, child?" *Affirmative*. "All right then. Now I'm going to teach you how to fight."

We've been at it for years. Many of those lessons will be shared through these pages. I'm no expert, but I'm willing to share the little I know. I believe with all my heart that if God can teach this former captive how to walk in victory and win horrific battles through the power of His Spirit, He can teach anyone.

Now that countless letters, frantic phone calls, and face-to-face testimonies have found their way to my office, I realize I am far from the only true lover of God whom Satan has tried to devour. Although I would never characterize myself as "godly," I will tell you that I loved God more than anything on earth at the times of greatest demonic assault.

I know plenty of others whom I would not hesitate to have called godly, yet they suddenly found themselves the object of an overwhelming assault of ungodliness. Oh yes, it can happen. In fact, I can't help but think Peter's words in 1 Peter 5:9 may apply to our generation like never before: "Your brothers throughout the world are undergoing the same kind of sufferings." Based on the findings landing on my desk, increasing numbers of dear brothers and sisters *throughout the world* are undergoing tremendous suffering at the paws of the roaring lion. Some of it comes in an unexpected, overwhelming season of temptation. Not unlike the temptations Satan hurled at Christ, they can vary in type, but one thing is for sure: They are tailor-made to catch the believer off guard. Many sincere believers fall before they even know what hit them.

Can you imagine the horror and isolation of devout missionaries on the foreign field who stumble into well-disguised traps of the devil? What do they do? Where do they go? Will people help? Or will they throw them out in disgrace? What's a Body to do with godly people who unexpectedly turn to ungodly things? May we give some very serious thought to the answers to these questions as we turn the pages of this book.

Charles Spurgeon provided a fitting conclusion to our first chapter. Read it soberly:

> There is nothing that Satan can do for his evil
> cause that he does not do. We may be halfhearted,
> but he never is. He is the very image of ceaseless
> industry and untiring earnestness. He will do all
> that can be done in the time of his permitted rage.
> We may be sure that he will never lose a day.[2]

Dear Body of Christ, it's time we put down the popguns of yesteryear's church. Satan is waging a worldwide nuclear war.

CHAPTER 2

SATAN'S WELL-
ATTENDED COURSE

As we study Scripture together throughout the chapters of this book, we are probably going to discover that Satan is far more powerful, personal, and conniving than many of us thought. Let's be very careful, however, not to dream of giving Satan more credit than he is due. While he is tremendously potent, armed, and dangerous, he is not the equal of the Most High God.

The Lord of hosts maintains authority over all powers and principalities. Satan is merely a created being. That doesn't mean the evil one is not a threat. At our strongest moments we are no match for him. The Almighty Three-in-One is the only one who can overpower Satan. We walk in the victory Christ won for us *only* when we are "strong in the Lord and in his mighty power" (Eph. 6:10).

A good time has come for a little background check on our enemy. Christ Himself referred to Satan as the prince of this world system in John 12:31 and 16:11. He also portrayed Satan as already defeated (Luke 10:18). So why is a defeated enemy so hard at work in a post-Calvary world? Perhaps this illustration will help.

In the United States our presidential elections occur in November, but the new president does not assume his position until January. Let's see if I can explain the parallel. I believe in a literal reign of Christ on this earth. I am convinced Scripture teaches that Christ Jesus will visibly return to earth and rule in righteousness for a thousand years. I also believe that the "scroll" described in Revelation 5 is somewhat of a title deed to the world system. God permitted that authority to fall into Satan's hands for a time, after man's forced exodus from the Garden. One day soon God will place that title deed back in the hands of its rightful ruler. At the God-ordained time, Christ will return to earth, conquer every foe, and take His seat of authority.

We now live in the period leading up to Christ taking His rightful throne. Today Christ is Lord of lords and King of kings, but His Kingdom is currently not of this world (see John 18:36). The day is coming when the nature of the Kingdom will change. The Christ who reigns today in believers will reign outwardly and absolutely. He will take back what the enemy has stolen.

As if Satan needed any more reason to rage, his situation becomes even more bleak. Peter described the consummation of the age in these words:

> The heavens will disappear with a roar; the
> elements will be destroyed by fire, and the earth
> and everything in it will be laid bare. . . . That day
> will bring about the destruction of the heavens by
> fire, and the elements will melt in the heat. But in
> keeping with his promise we are looking forward

to a new heaven and a new earth, the home of
righteousness. (2 Pet. 3:10, 12–13)

Don't miss the significance of Peter's words from Satan's perspective. All beings will be in their eternal state from this time forward—whether redeemed in the presence of God or unredeemed
in the lake of fire (Rev. 20:15). Think soberly of those words: *no
other place will exist.* Satan rages because he knows his eternal destiny bears down on him like an approaching freight train, and he
is out of options.

The thought of the future of the unredeemed makes me
shiver. I have no desire for *anyone* to go there. Not even the vilest
sinner. I pray for *all* to repent! If God was willing to save me, He
is willing to save anyone who asks. He does not want "anyone to
perish, but everyone to come to repentance" (2 Pet. 3:9).

In my illustration, election day took place on the cross. Christ
has the only valid claim as the ultimate ruler of all creation. That's
why the apostle John saw

a Lamb, looking as if it had been slain, standing in
the center of the throne, encircled by the four living creatures and the elders. . . . He came and
took the scroll from the right hand of him who sat
on the throne. (Rev. 5:6–7)

The one on the throne is God, of course. He is the all-
powerful, ultimate ruler of heaven and earth, and nothing happens except by His perfect or permissive will. Yes, Satan has been
"prince of this world," but only by divine permissive will and to

accomplish God's own purposes. Satan was completely defeated by the offering of the perfect, sinless life of the Son of God on the cross. One day Christ will assume full reign of the world system where Satan has wreaked such havoc. Presently, however, the world exists in the period between the new election and the earthly inauguration of Christ.

Suppose we had a wicked president who knew he had already been defeated in the election and his removal from office was imminent. Can you imagine how he might wield and abuse his power in the little time he had left? On a mammoth, humanly incomprehensible scale, I believe that's what we're presently experiencing.

Satan reads the signs of the times like the *Washington Post.* He knows the inauguration of Christ's kingdom grows closer and closer, so the archdemon furiously unleashes his power to the full extent of God's permissive will. The dragon is in a tailspin, and he is whipping everything he can in the time he has left. Because his ultimate fury is at God, nothing gives Satan greater unholy pleasure than assaulting God's children. Hence, our present conflict.

Our purpose through this book then is to understand how the people described in 2 Corinthians 11:2–3 as being *wholeheartedly, sincerely, and purely devoted to Christ* can be beguiled by Satan and have their minds *corrupted and seduced.*

Certainly no one will argue that a believer can be characterized as godly while practicing ungodly things. Our task is to understand how a person who has consistently walked with God can be so powerfully seduced to ungodliness.

If I were forced to put an entire concept in a nutshell, I'd have to say that somewhere along the way, the godly person walked into a well-spun lie. Lies are Satan's stock in trade. He "fathers" every deception (John 8:44) and seduction (2 Cor. 11:2–3), but he does not personally carry out all of them. Satan is not omnipresent as is our God. On the contrary, Satan can only be in one place at a time.

Satan has a massive number of unholy hosts who carry out his purposes. Psalm 91:11–12 and Hebrews 1:14 talk about angels that God assigns to minister to His children in certain ways. Angels were never meant to distract us from the worship of God, but their activity in our lives appears biblically legitimate. Keep in mind that Satan is the ultimate counterfeiter. Anything God *yup!* does, Satan attempts to counterfeit.

All along, Satan has been trying to make himself "like the Most High" (Isa. 14:14). I would not be at all surprised if he counterfeits God's appointment of angels to every believer by appointing demons to every believer. In this way, we all become targets of Satan's temptations and works of destruction, yet not often by Satan himself. Rather, we must usually deal with the demons sent to do his bidding.

The Word of God often refers to demonic spirits as *unclean spirits.* Here we have a critical clue to Satan's objective in the life of a believer. When we receive Christ, we are made *clean.* As far-fetched as this may seem to us at times, the Word of God unashamedly calls the redeemed of Christ *saints* or *holy ones.* Ephesians 5:25–26 tells us that

> Christ loved the church and gave himself up
> for her to make her holy, cleansing her by the
> washing with water through the word, and to

present her to himself as a radiant church, without
stain or wrinkle or any other blemish, but holy
and blameless.

Satan so vehemently despises what Christ has done for mortals that one of his chief objectives is to make the clean *feel* unclean. Oh, how he desires to stain the beautiful bride of Christ. Satan can't *make* the bride do anything, so he does everything he can to *get* her to. How is this best accomplished? He tries to corrupt thoughts to manipulate feelings.

Satan knows that the nature of humankind is to act out of how we feel rather than what we know. One of our most important defenses against satanic influence will be learning how to behave out of what we know is *truth* rather than what we feel.

Satan's desire is to modify human behavior to accomplish his unholy purposes. Second Timothy 2:26 tells us that Satan's objective in taking people captive is to get them to do *his will*. If we have received Christ as our Savior, Satan is forced to work from the outside rather than the inside. Thus, he manipulates outside influences to affect the inside decision-makers of the heart and mind. We'll learn far more about how to recognize his schemes later in this book.

We have just arrived at the primary reason why one of Satan's most powerful weapons is sexual seduction. Remember, he wants to make the clean feel unclean in hopes that they will act unclean.

Please don't think for a moment that all seduction is sexually oriented. Most assuredly it is not. Believers can be seduced by power, by money, by position, by false doctrine, or by any number of flesh-fueling pumps.

Few things, however, accomplish Satan's goal of inducing feelings and actions of uncleanness in those who are clean like sexual seduction. Somehow Satan makes sure it just seems dirtier than the rest of the dirt. He also likes to instigate falls that carry long-term effects. Sexual sin is a perfect choice to achieve his goals. It is can be highly addictive. It breeds shame like nothing else and has uniquely horrendous ramifications. First Corinthians 6:18–20 explains why:

> Flee from sexual immorality. All other sins a
> man commits are outside his body, but he who
> sins sexually sins against his own body. Do you
> not know that your body is a temple of the Holy
> Spirit, who is in you, whom you have received
> from God? You are not your own; you were
> bought at a price. Therefore honor God with your
> body.

In *Praying God's Word,* God directed me to address the powerful yoke of sexually oriented bondage. I'd like to share a slice of something He revealed to me as I researched the reasons why sexual strongholds are so potent and satanically effective.

> Satan desires to undermine the sanctifying
> work of Christ. He knows that all believers have
> been "set apart" from the unclean to the clean, and
> from the unholy to the holy. He also knows that
> when believers act like the sanctified people they
> are, God is released to do powerful wonders

23

among them (Josh. 3:5). No purity—no power. Purity—boundless power. Satan is a fool but he is no dummy.

Satan knows the overwhelming effects of sexual sin. We must resist "ranking" sin since every sin causes us to miss the mark and require grace. All sin is equal in the sense of eternal ramifications, but not all sin is equal in its earthly ramifications. Satan knows that sexual sin is unique in its attack and impact on the body of the individual believer. . . . Since the Spirit of Christ now dwells in the temple of believers' bodies, getting a Christian engaged in sexual sin is the closest Satan can come to personally assaulting Christ. That ought to make us mad enough to be determined to live victoriously. Sins against the body also have a way of sticking to us and making us feel like we *are* that sin rather than the fact that we've *committed* that sin.[1]

Stealing is a sin, yet if I stole one hundred dollars and then changed my mind, dumping the money in a garbage bin, in some respects I could walk away without taking the "sin" with me. On the other hand, if I commit sexual sin, I have a much harder time dumping the garbage. Why? Because spiritually speaking, it got "on" me somehow. The sin was against my own body and wields a much stronger staying power.

Sexual sin can be dumped, all right, but not in a garbage bin. Only Christ through the power of His cross can peel off the adhesive effects of sexual sin. The sin against the body somewhat resembles the outer layer of skin on a burn victim. It must be peeled off, and fresh new skin must be allowed to grow. Satan cannot get inside a believer, but sexual seduction is one of the most powerful ways the fires of hell can burn the outside of a believer. The sin is forgiven the moment the person repents, but healing from the ramifications can take longer.

God desires more than anything to restore sexual purity to those who have been sexually seduced, but it takes time to peel away the damaged character. The pain that can be involved in the process demands much trust in a good and loving God.

Beloved, trusting God is utterly essential if we are going to fortify our lives. Through the chapters of this book and the co-inciding study of Scripture, we're going to discover that our safety resides in withholding absolutely nothing in us or about us from God.

If we searched for the root of our seasons of sin, we would find that a disastrous harvest almost always has its beginning in a deeply imbedded seed of distrust. Some level of unbelief is involved in every sin. That's how Paul could make such a bold, all-inclusive statement in Romans 14:23: "Everything that does not come from faith is sin."

In his book *Ruthless Trust,* Brennan Manning wrote:

> Alas, another form of tainted trust is dis-
> honesty with Jesus. Sometimes we harbor an un-
> expressed suspicion that he cannot handle all that
> goes on in our minds and hearts. We doubt that
> he can accept our hateful thoughts, cruel fantasies,

and bizarre dreams. We wonder how he would deal with our primitive urges, our inflated illusions, and our exotic mental castles. The deep resistance to making ourselves so vulnerable, so naked, so totally unprotected is our implicit way of saying, "Jesus, I trust you, but there are limits."

By refusing to share our fantasies, worries, and joys, we limit God's lordship over our life and make clear that there are parts of us that we do not wish to submit to divine conversation.

It seems that the Master had something more in mind when he said, "Trust in me."[2]

Brick by brick, God builds a mighty fortress around our lives as we learn to bring to the light (through open dialogue with God) that which we by human nature leave in the dark. Beloved, we must learn to trust God with our sexuality. Fig leaves wouldn't hide Adam and Eve from God. Our modern forms of fig leaves won't protect us from the enemy. Surely it's more than coincidental that Satan is having his greatest field day over the very dimension of our lives that we are most reluctant to bring before God for help, healing, and wholeness.

We discussed the approaching end of the age as a reason for the rising phenomenon of godly people being enticed to ungodly things. Christ referenced the "increase of wickedness" as one of the signs of the end of the age and His coming (Matt. 24:12).

I'm not sure we have any greater evidence that we are entering the latter days than the incomprehensible mushrooming of sexual sin. According to the cover story of the March 2000

Online U.S. News entitled "A Lust for Profit," "Web surfers spent $970 million on the access to adult-content sites in 1998, according to the research from Datamonitor, and that figure could rise to more than $3 billion by 2003." The article also claims that "with the dot-comming of America near complete, salacious fare remains a huge—and growing—cyberspace draw. According to Nielson NetRatings, 17.5 million surfers visited porn sites from their homes in January [2000], a 40 percent increase compared with four months earlier.[3]

In an article entitled "Devastated by Internet Porn," writer Steve Gallagher of Pure Life Ministries cited an even more troubling statistic. "Tragically, the percentage of Christian men involved is not much different than that of the unsaved. According to a survey of pastors and lay leaders conducted by *Leadership Magazine*, 62% have regularly viewed pornography."[4]

As we consider how godly people can be enticed into doing ungodly things, please keep in mind that religious position and godliness are not synonymous. Neither guarantees the other. We can certainly be in church leadership positions without ever having a pure and wholehearted devotion to Christ. The horrible tragedy is how many among those statistics may have formerly lived godly lives. What happened to them? And what happens to them now? That's what you and I are trying to find out as we make our way through these pages.

In 1 Timothy 4:1 Paul made a statement pertinent to our present subject matter: "But the (Holy) Spirit distinctly and expressly declares that in latter times some will turn away from the faith, giving attention to deluding and seducing spirits and doctrines that demons teach" (AMP).

In Paul and Timothy's day, one of the most common demonic doctrines was a strictly denial-based lifestyle banning marriage and certain foods, all of which were created by God to be enjoyed. Satan's objective was to fuel the flesh by denying it the very things God had ordained. I don't think Paul ever intended the reader to assume that the only doctrines of demons were the ones he mentioned in his first letter to Timothy. He simply pointed out the ones that were most prevalent in their world.

In our society, Satan is empowering his evil spirits for the express purpose of seduction, hoping to lead many to turn away from the faith. These demons may "teach" any number of ungodly doctrines, but perhaps the demonic professors with the best-attended classes are those that teach the demonic doctrine of abstaining from nothing at all.

Seduction can take many different forms, but Satan is no doubt having an illicit field day by sexually seducing many saints. Do you see what he has done through what has now been dubbed *E-porn?* Not nearly enough believers were coming to him for pornography, so he simply brought it to them. Home delivery. As close as the click of a mouse. It's ingenious, really. Pastors and lay leaders who have never in their lives bought an illicit magazine are suddenly falling under a huge wave of temptation to look "just once" at a pornographic Web site.

In Steve Gallagher's article, he tells about a pastor by the name of Jessie who fell into an unplanned, overpowering addiction to pornography.

> Pastor Jessie's story is fairly common. Upon completing Bible College, he entered ministry with a

sincere desire to "walk in a manner pleasing to the Lord." At first, he maintained a healthy relationship with God, ministering to his flock out of the spiritual abundance that came from his vibrant devotional life. Eventually people began flocking to his church. This taste of success drove Jessie on. As his ever-increasing responsibilities demanded more of his time, his prayer life began to dwindle. When he did try to pray, heaven seemed closed to him. Rather than spending time in the Word seeking the spiritual nourishment he needed personally, he simply spent his time looking for sermon material. Over a period of months, the fountain of life had dried up for him. True, his ministry continued to flourish, but inwardly he was growing increasingly apathetic and cold hearted.

Jessie didn't realize it, but his spiritual listlessness made him an open target for the enemy. During this period of time, he began having occasional lustful thoughts. At first, he would shut them out, but as time went on, he increasingly entertained them. One day, while on the Internet, the thought came to him to type a sexual phrase into the search engine. With a mounting curiosity and a depleted spiritual life, he gave in to the temptation . . . he spent two hours rushing through dozens of adult websites. Jessie had just entered the dark realm of pornography.

Over the next several months, this once-godly-man plunged deeper and deeper into the sewers of perverted images. He kept telling himself that he would quit, not realizing that every single visit to a porn site was digging him into a deeper pit that would be harder to climb out of. Getting caught by his wife was a beginning, but he had developed a serious addiction by this time."[5]

My heart broke as I read this statement in the article: "The look of horror and betrayal on her face when she saw the computer screen would haunt him for months to come." Jessie has more company than any of us would like to imagine.

The number of believers who had never before viewed pornography then nearly smothered to death under its life-crushing heap is escalating beyond our wildest imaginations. Perhaps out of curiosity. Perhaps out of loneliness. Perhaps to feel passion again. Perhaps as a way to do mentally what many think they would dare not do physically—a very foolish assumption and one that has proved erroneous many times. Satan has gained a gargantuan victory either way. More often than not, "just once" turns into "just twice." Then three times, four times, and a believer who once walked with God in purity has just developed the fiercest addiction of his or her entire life. Everything is effected. The marriage. The children. The workplace. The ministry.

Of course, Satan already knew that. It went exactly as he planned. It doesn't have to keep going his way, though. His ultimate goal is that people follow the seducing spirits so far that they "turn away from the faith" (1 Tim. 4:1 AMP). If this sounds familiar to you and you are beginning to recognize that you have been powerfully seduced into the demonic doctrine of sexual perversion, don't turn away from the faith! Turn back! That's what Jessie finally did, but he had the fight of his life on his hands, and the path of destruction behind him was violent.

Satan will do everything he can to hang on once he gets a foothold in us. Don't wait another minute! The longer a person waits to cry out for deliverance and cooperate with God, the tighter the grip grows on the yoke. If Satan has you in chains and you want out, the entire third portion of this book is dedicated to your full return and to the return of others, no matter what sort of yoke binds you or them.

As we draw this chapter to conclusion, I am compelled once again to shout from the rooftops what I've already said in several other books: The Body of Christ is being sexually assaulted by the devil! We must learn how to defend ourselves in the power of God's Word and His Spirit.

Just as we teach our young daughters how to guard themselves against sexual assaults, the Body has got to be taught how to guard her virginity. Oh, that the church would start dealing openly and honestly with crimes against the Body. It's time we dump the denial, pick up the Sword of the Spirit, and learn how to use it. *Oh, God, please help us. We are under such attack. Far too many believers who have histories of faithfulness with You are falling for the devil's schemes. Please open our eyes and show us the way! Hear the desperate cries of Your children.*

CHAPTER 3

COMMON CLAIMS
OF THE SEDUCED

I f this book had been written by someone else and I were reading it, I'd be asking more than a few questions. To name a few:
"Are you suggesting that all godly people can be enticed by the
enemy to do ungodly things? Is no one safe? And, if that's what
you're saying, why do some people walk faithfully with God all
their believing lives without ever departing into ungodliness?"
Good questions, if I do say so myself.

Let's examine each question. First, what about susceptibility?
While all of us have the *capability* of departing into ungodliness,
not all share the same degree of risk. Thankfully, some believers
have so wholly allowed their bodies, souls, and spirits to be sanctified to the authority of Christ that they will have a strong, successful defense against seducing spirits. We'll talk more about that
critical process in part 2, but I certainly wanted to set the record
straight before we get there. No, not everyone will fall for seducing
spirits, and, yes, some believers walk faithfully with God all their
believing lives without departing into absolute ungodliness.

Oh, I wish I had been one of them! The fact is, I'm not. I surrendered to vocational ministry at the age of eighteen with a genuine love for God and a desire to serve Him faithfully all the days of my life. Yet I had already broken virtually every promise I made to Him by the time I was twenty! I am so grateful God didn't break His promises to me.

I did not plan to veer from the path. Nothing could have been further from my mind. I loved God with every ounce of my handicapped heart. If I had known then what I know now, I would have known I was a devout young woman sitting pretty for seduction. I had several tangles with the devil before I allowed God to teach me how to defend myself. I hate some of the places I've been and ways I had to learn, but I am here to testify that I am no longer easy prey.

If I hadn't danced with the devil several times in my life, I certainly wouldn't be writing this book. We go on in life with what we each have. I don't have a spotless track record, and I choose the liberty of not even pretending that I do. But what I do have is experience.

Satan hopes our horrible experiences will cause us to live in the past. *No way*—this pilgrim is moving forward, but I keep my experience tucked in my backpack. It serves to warn me along my way and to be of any help to another sojourner. I'm not sure I could have read this book from someone who hadn't been there. If I hadn't experienced some of the very things I'm about to tell you others have, I would be inclined to think that much of what we're about to discuss was—how shall I say it?—*hogwash*.

In chapter 1, I told you how my concern grew out of reading a stack of unnerving testimonials from people who had devoted their lives to Christ and walked with God consistently for an extended period of time only to be suddenly seduced into ungodly behavior. I knew I was looking at the very essence of 2 Corinthians 11:2–3. I poured over their stories with great attention and growing alarm, all the while asking God to give me discernment. As I read their stories and reflected on my own, I kept thinking, *Do you know how many Christians don't believe this is possible?*

I have since made a case study of sorts out of many of their experiences. I met with a substantial number of them face-to-face, *not* as a counselor but as a researcher. I asked some hard questions and got what I believe were some very honest answers.

I never failed to be amazed at the brilliant schemes of the devil and was floored by his ability to take advantage of well-hidden weaknesses. In this chapter you will find a list of common claims and common denominators from these persons' experiences.

By no means am I suggesting that all seductions share these commonalities. We have no idea how many shapes, sizes, and forms seductions can take. I have been shocked, however, by a number of common claims that I think are worth our notice. I have three reasons I consider exceedingly important for sharing them with you.

1. If you love someone or you're counseling someone who is making similar claims, you need to know that many others have described the same things. Your loved one or your client may not be crazy after all! They may be beguiled!

2. I am hoping and praying with all my heart that someone who is presently being seduced may pick up this book and use the

following claims as a checklist of sorts to recognize their seduction. Recognition can be the first sign of "light" in this dark encounter.

Please don't think for a second that if one or two of these common denominators don't fit, you are not being seduced. I'm certain this list is incomplete and inconclusive. I would have kept compiling data except that God explicitly told me that I had plenty and to get busy writing this message. If the majority of these fit, beloved, you are most likely being seduced. Cry out to God with everything that is in you! Remember, you can't trust your feelings, so if you don't "feel" like you "want" to be rescued, reason with yourself and admit that you "need" to be rescued. Lastly, keep in mind that some of the common claims came in the aftermath of the seduction, so if you are still actively in the stronghold of seduction, you haven't experienced them yet.

3. If you've been through a similar nightmare and have told no one, it's time you had a name for it. Dear one, you've been seduced.

One last reminder before we begin the list. Please remember not to assume that all seduction is sexual in nature. After our last chapter, you might be inclined to read it into every story. Please think far more widely as you try to grasp the breadth of Satan's expertise. Remember, he's simply after whatever works. In fact, one of the most intriguing aspects of the common claims I began to tally was the variance of schemes the enemy used from person to person. What intertwined their lives, unknown to them, was a testimony of having walked consistently and lovingly with God for some time only to suddenly enter a season of uncharacteristic behavior they considered ungodly.

Those who were enticed to do ungodly things after living godly lives shared many of the following sixteen claims:

1. They were caught off guard by a sudden onslaught of temptation or attack.

Not one of these individuals planned their season of ungodliness. Virtually all of them felt as if they were hit so hard and so fast that their heads were spinning. Many described having already sinned before they even knew what hit them. Sound impossible? Actually, the possibility is stated unapologetically in Scripture. Galatians 6:1 says, "Brothers, if someone is caught in a sin, you who are spiritual should restore him gently. But watch yourself, or you also may be tempted." Concentrate on the word *caught*. One of the definitions of the Greek word *prolambano* describes the sin like this: "catches the individual by surprise, suddenly, without notice, i.e., before he is aware of what has happened."[1] In fact, the *pro* in *prolambano* means "before."

We would not be abandoning sound theology to say that these kinds of sins can overtake someone before he realizes what is coming against him and puts his guard up. Several other versions translate *caught* as "overtaken." After catching his prey off guard, then the enemy does all he can to make the victim feel completely trapped, but as we'll discover, he can't keep up the façade indefinitely.

Most of those who contacted me would never have believed they were capable of some of their actions. Their testimonies weren't those of chasing after sin in proactive rebellion. Rather, they reacted wrongfully and sinfully to something that I believe was a *seduction*.

As we delineate between sin of rebellion and sin as the result of seduction, please understand that it is *all* iniquity and requires

God's graceful forgiveness. Also understand that while many informative books speak to sins of rebellion, this one deals with sins resulting from seduction. The same grace covers all, but the Body of Christ isn't ill-informed about rebellion nearly as much as we are about seduction. We *know* the rebellious can get into big trouble, but we're desperate to wake up to the fact that the godly can find themselves in trouble too.

2. The season of overwhelming temptation and seduction often followed huge spiritual markers with God.

These godly people who then did ungodly things were not walking in sin when the wave of seduction hit. I was amazed how many felt they had just entered a new season of growth in their relationships with God—if not a near spiritual euphoria—when the unimaginable happened.

After giving it some thought, it makes perfect sense. The devil wants to stop any believer from fulfilling his or her God-given destiny. He also knows that most believers feel almost invulnerable after a mountaintop experience with God. Actually, that's when we are most vulnerable because falling into sin is the last thing we're expecting. We're wise to expect times of testing after times of blessing.

Remember, Christ Himself endured a dreadful time of testing after receiving great blessing. After He was baptized by John, He heard the glorious words from His Father in heaven: "This is my Son, whom I love; with Him I am well pleased." The very next words? "Then Jesus was led by the Spirit into the desert to be tempted by the devil."

Of course, Jesus endured His season of temptation without sin, but the experience was inconceivably brutal. Please hear this, child of God. Colossians 2:9 tells us Christ was the bodily fullness of the Godhead. If anyone has ever been the epitome of godliness in human flesh, it was He! Yet, He was dogged ferociously by the devil after the spiritual pinnacle of His incarnation to that point.

Knowing all that would come upon us, our faithful God met every provision, even in our temptation. "For we do not have a high priest who is unable to sympathize with our weaknesses, but we have one who has been tempted in every way, just as we are— yet was without sin. Let us then approach the throne of grace with confidence, so that we may receive mercy and find grace to help us in our time of need" (Heb. 4:15–16).

3. Everyone described a mental bombardment.

Another way to describe the same thing is *obsessive thinking*. This one isn't hard to understand. Indeed, it is one of the clearest signs of a fierce demonic stronghold.

Remember our key verse? Second Corinthians 11:2–3 specifically states that the believer can be devoted to Christ with his whole heart, yet Satan can "corrupt" and "seduce" his (or her) *mind*. In the previous chapter of Scripture, Paul had just described a stronghold:

> For though we walk in the flesh, we do not
> war after the flesh: (For the weapons of our
> warfare are not carnal, but mighty through God to
> the pulling down of strong holds;) Casting down

imaginations, and every high thing that exalteth
itself against the knowledge of God, and bringing
into captivity every thought to the obedience of
Christ. (2 Cor. 10:3–5 KJV)

The very nature of a stronghold is that something is exalted
in our minds contrary to the knowledge of God. Breaking free
from these mentally obsessive strongholds always requires bringing those previously exalted imaginations into the captivity of
Christ's authority. No small challenge—one the enemy hopes
we're not "up to." We have to prove him wrong. We have *divine
power to demolish strongholds.* Only in our own power is the task
too much for us.

4. Many of those caught in relational seductions (not all seductions are relational) testified that Satan got to them through someone close by.

When Satan is trying to wreak havoc on the godly, he isn't
always successful with a blatantly ungodly approach. Remember,
we're talking seduction here. The nature of seduction implies an
unexpected, well-disguised lure. Satan looks for ways he can get
close to the godly and gain trust.

The last thing I want to do is suggest that we cease trusting
people, but be warned that not everyone who appears trustworthy *is.* Perhaps we've all had times when we weren't terribly
trustworthy ourselves. Again, we should be desperate for discernment and, thankfully, God is willing to supply it. In part 2 we will
talk about safeguarding relationships. Part of our fortification

against seduction will be making sure a door has not been opened in our lives through an unhealthy relationship.

5. Many testified to early warning signals.

Not surprising, of course. The Holy Spirit does not fail to do His job. Over and over I have asked, "Did you ever get a 'flag' of some kind that caused you to think you ought not to proceed in that relationship or situation?" Almost invariably every one of them said yes. It came while they were still walking faithfully with God. I asked why they didn't heed the warning, and virtually all of them said they rationalized it away.

One woman told me that she thought it was her own flesh nature resisting someone who needed help, and she rationalized that the godly thing to do was show mercy. Actually, the Holy Spirit was telling her to run for her life from an unrepentant person momentarily being manipulated by the devil.

Again, do you see how much we need discernment? Sometimes we get a gut feeling that we ought to avoid involvement in a situation, and sometimes that gut feeling is the work of the Holy Spirit. We will fall under criticism at times for backing out of a situation simply because something we can't define doesn't seem just right. Better to be criticized, however, than fall for a demonic scheme.

6. Many described their sudden behavioral patterns as totally uncharacteristic.

I can't tell you the number of times I have heard the following statements: "I kept thinking, *What in the world am I doing? I have never acted like this in my life!"* Most mentioned that family, close friends, and associates also noticed uncharacteristic behavior. Anyone who confronted them, however, was met with defensiveness and rationalizations.

I have a clear memory from many years ago that still dumbfounds me. I remember unleashing a sudden string of curse words. What made it so peculiar is that I honestly don't curse. Trust me. I've done much worse, but I've just never been given to a foul mouth. I don't have an especially irate personality. I remember staring at myself in the mirror later and thinking, *Who in the world are you? I don't even know you.* The feeling was so weird. Of course, it was me all right. I was not possessed by the devil, but I don't mind telling you that I was temporarily under the most powerfully oppressive influence I've ever encountered.

7. Virtually all of them described feelings and practices of isolation.

Satan's temptation of Christ is certainly not the only example of isolation. The Old Testament prophet Elijah fell into a terrible time of depression in isolation after a vivid mountaintop experience with God.

Satan loves isolation. He wants to draw the believer out of healthy relationships into isolated relationships and out of healthy practices into secretive, unhealthy practices. He purposely woos us away from those who might openly recognize the seduction and call his hand on it. Let's beware of anything that separates us from godly people.

Hebrews 10:24–25 is more than a sweet little feel-good Scripture. Read these two verses in context with our present subject matter:

> And let us consider how we may spur one
> another on to love and good deeds. Let us not give
> up meeting together, as some are in the habit of
> doing, but let us encourage one another—and all
> the more as you see the Day approaching.

What "Day" is he talking about? The Day of the Lord! In other words, exactly what Christ was talking about in His discourse on the signs of His coming and the end of the age. Why must we encourage one another all the more as the time hastens? Because of the increase in deception, wickedness, and seduction! We need one another more than ever! Knowing that we do, Satan's reasons for encouraging isolation are obvious.

8. Without exception, deception and some level of secrecy are involved.

Once again, remember that the "secret power of lawlessness is already at work." Satan loves secrets and often works through disguises, masquerades, and shrouds. He wants things to stay in the dark because he knows the moment we expose it to the light of God, he's finished.

Deception is an absolute in every stronghold, but the nature of *seductive* deception is that the lies are often well masked for a while. We are undoubtedly caught in a stronghold of deception when we realize we're starting to "have to lie" to explain our behavior. We reason with ourselves that others just wouldn't understand, but the real reason is that the deceived soon deceive.

9. Many described overwhelming feelings of powerlessness.

The feeling being fueled is a lie, of course, and a perfect example of a doctrine of demons. Believers are only powerless in their own strength, and God has promised to provide a way of escape for every temptation. The power of seduction is indescribable, however. Not inescapable, nor totally irresistible, but indescribable.

If you've never been hit by a satanic tidal wave, you're inclined to think that walking away from any sin is a matter of making a simple decision. You may never have experienced the feeling of being completely overpowered. Again, we see that Satan's attempt is to inspire a feeling so strong it eclipses the truth. The next common denominator could be one major reason why seduction is not so easy to walk away from.

10. Many described something we'll call an "addictive nature" to the seductive sin.

Mind you, they can't fully explain some of the things they felt in the heat of the battle any more than I can explain how I felt in times of my own severest warfare. I'm not saying anyone fully understands it. I just asked them to try to describe it. I'm bringing to the table what was told by completely independent sources who didn't know anyone else had said something similar.

Not long ago I heard a Christian psychologist say that people can be addicted to other people in unhealthy relationships. At this point, I'm becoming more and more convinced that this "addiction" to a person or a behavior as opposed to a habit-forming substance could be the work of a seducing spirit and not simply an emotional malady. Certainly, Satan targets our emotions because our hearts are by their own nature deceptive (Jer. 17:9). Most assuredly, where believers are concerned, the father of lies is at the heart of every destructive emotional tie.

11. Most utterly hated what they were doing.

In all probability, this characteristic is somehow connected to the previous one. Someone extremely dear to me has battled alcoholism for years and is finally winning the battle. She despised what she was doing but felt powerless to stop. The addiction was overwhelming. Similarly, almost every person I interviewed testified that they hated their ungodly behavior but for a season were drawn like a magnet to it.

Part of Satan's ploy is to make his victims "feel" addicted and powerless. Sometimes the seduction so corrupts the mind and confuses the feelings that it draws off of the pure animal-like instinct of the flesh. The seduced person often deplores what she's doing but in the heat of the battle feels overpowered by it. Sometimes people can describe a time of rebellion with a mischievous grin and even admit to having enjoyed it. But I have never heard a godly person seduced by the enemy say they could look back on the time with a smile. All will tell you it was their worst nightmare. It filled their lives with shame, and they ended up being sickened by it.

12. The seduction lasted only for a season.

Needless to say, the time frames varied, but people with a genuine heart for God cannot remain in a practice of sin. At some point they will cry out in total desperation for deliverance. For those who have walked closely with God, the desire for a return to His intimate favor finally exceeds the lure of their seducer. In the end, Satan cannot cut it because he can't continue to sustain it. Those who have known the truth will finally recognize the lie.

First John 3:9 says, "No one who is born of God will continue to sin, because God's seed remains in him; he cannot go on sinning, because he has been born of God." John makes a similar statement in 1 John 5:18, then says something that seems in our English understanding totally to contradict the claims this book is making: "We know that anyone born of God does not continue to sin; the one who was born of God keeps him safe, and the evil one cannot harm him." The King James Version goes so far as to say "that wicked one toucheth him not." I'm not sure either word, *harm* or *touch*, adequately expresses the original. I'm going to let Charles Ryrie explain this one out of his fine work entitled *Basic Theology:*

> It means not a superficial touching but a
> grasping, clinging to, or holding on to someone.
> Satan can never hang on to the believer with the
> purpose of harming him, for that believer belongs
> eternally and irrevocably to God. Satan (or
> demons) may afflict and even control for a time
> but never permanently or eternally.[2]

With this explanation in mind, perhaps the Amplified Bible words it best:

> We know [absolutely] that any one born of
> God does not [deliberately and knowingly] prac-
> tice committing sin, but the One Who was begot-
> ten of God carefully watches over and protects
> him—Christ's divine presence within him pre-
> serves him against the evil—and the wicked one
> does not lay hold (get a grip) on him or touch
> [him]. (1 John 5:18)

Satan cannot possessively lay hold of us, keep us in a grip, or touch us in a way that will utterly destroy us. We may "feel" destroyed, but we are not. Christ will preserve us from Satan's ultimate intent—our total destruction.

The next three common claims of the seduced call for a preface. Like most of you, I prefer to study facts rather than feelings, and I'm aware that we are wavering at times in this chapter between the objective and the subjective. Let me say something, however, on behalf of many victims of seduction. Each feels like he or she is the only one in the Christian world who has ever sincerely loved God and fallen into such uncharacteristic and even horrifying sin.

Because God chose to supply me with so much unsolicited data, I have learned something they may not know: *They are not the only ones.* Many have been through the same kinds of experiences and even felt the same inexplicable things. They are not alone and they need to know it. For that reason, I want to share the feelings they described whether or not the reader thinks they are legitimate. I am not asking you to believe them. I am asking you to "hear" them.

If you disagree on my choice to mention these common claims, I ask you to consider not discarding the whole book because you cannot swallow a small portion of it. Please give the entire message prayerful consideration. Totally unrelated people describing some of the exact same experiences should at least cause us to consider. Let's respect them enough to hear them out.

13. Many describe a period of a spiritual numbness of sorts.

Perhaps because they are in such a state of shock and seduction, they often report not feeling the expected feelings of immediate devastation. Many reported that "it just didn't seem real for a while." I'm not sure how Satan does it, but I think he does everything he can to suspend godly sorrow. Why? That one's easy! Because godly sorrow brings repentance (2 Cor. 7:10), and he wants to delay repentance as long as possible. He keeps his victims so fueled with other confusing feelings that they often report not feeling what was real. Jesus Jesus

Needless to say, the victim has also resisted the warnings of the Holy Spirit and finally quenched Him enough that the normal spiritual feelings are temporarily diluted. Satan may work enough confusion to be able to delay feelings of repentance for a little while, but he cannot have his way for long. To anyone who has ever truly loved God, those feelings come all right. And when they finally come, the sorrow is almost unbearable.

14. Many used the same peculiar word to describe what they had experienced.

Over and over I have heard the word *web* coming from those trying to find a word to describe what they felt they had escaped. Keep in mind, they were not aware others were using the same word. We will take a better look at what this word probably represents in part 2 as we learn to fortify ourselves against seduction. We'll also discover a New Testament word that might help us characterize, visualize, and avoid weblike situations.

15. Many describe the aftermath as a time of slowly increasing awareness rather than an instant "wake up."

I am aware that I am going to lose some skeptics here, but I may as well go ahead and get it over with: Many people describe the season following their separation from the seducer like coming out from under the influence of a drug. You may be thinking they were making excuses for their behavior, but by the time most of these contacted me, they had already taken full responsibility for their sins and were blaming virtually no one but themselves.

No, they were not saying the devil "made" them do it, but they were saying that coming out from under the influence of this very powerful thing they couldn't define was like slowly getting a drug out of their system. The more they "woke up," the madder and sadder they became. I am so glad many of you have no idea what these people are talking about. Praise God! At the same time I will tell you that I believe what many are describing is authentic even if I can't adequately explain it for them.

Not only have I personally experienced the mind-bending effects of the devil during several profoundly difficult seasons, I have worked with several others on their ways "out" of seduction. I have had more experience with people strung out on drugs than I care to share, but when I met with one Christian young woman who had been trapped by the devil, I was flabbergasted by how much she looked like she had been on a drug binge. Her eyes were glassy, with terribly dark circles underneath. Her skin looked horrible. She looked like a skeleton and had completely lost her appetite—yet she was as drug-free as she could be. "All" she had done was tangle with the devil.

Of course, I also believe in the possibility of pure sin-sickness. Whatever the cause of this woman's terribly weakened physical state, I got to watch her recovery firsthand. Over the course of time, her former beauty not only was restored; it was entirely surpassed. The confusion in her mind was slowly replaced with truth. She returned to the lover of her soul and is God's woman in every sense of the Word.

I know! I know! We want Scriptures, not experientials, and rightly we should. Let's turn back to our original Scripture. Second Corinthians 11:3 states, "But [now] I am fearful lest that even as the serpent beguiled Eve by his cunning, so your minds may be corrupted and seduced from wholehearted and sincere and pure devotion to Christ" (AMP). This Scripture suggests that even the minds of those who were wholeheartedly devoted to Christ can be "corrupted" and "seduced." I don't think this is entirely unlike a brainwashing of sorts. (With sewer water, I might add.)

What do we think Satan is doing to the minds of those who have been seduced into religious cults? Someone might argue,

"But surely they were not Christians or they would have known better." On the contrary, many Christians have been swayed into bizarre doctrines that still employ the name of Christ.

God has been so gracious to broaden my concept of seduction and to teach me that it comes in many forms. We are quick to assume seduction is almost entirely sexual in nature, but as I've said, it is not. I have a *very* dear friend whose entire family was seduced by a religious cult that proclaimed Jesus as Savior but steered them away from their own study of the Word, interpreting Scripture to them in self-promoting ways. She and her husband were as saved as Billy Graham when they were snared into this cult and even became leaders in the "church."

These believers were talked into investing all their money into the false church and church-related businesses and lost every dime they had. They finally left the cult, but it was months and even years before they fully assimilated what they had been through and how terribly they had been seduced. Now it is so clear. Then it was so convincing.

I love the wording of the King James Version of 2 Corinthians 11:3: "But I fear, lest by any means, as the serpent beguiled Eve through his subtilty, so your minds should be corrupted from the simplicity that is in Christ." Note the word *simplicity*. In the original language, it means all the things the Amplified Bible suggests, but it also indicates the opposite of duplicity. James 1:8 gives a great definition of duplicity: "A double minded man is unstable in all his ways" (KJV).

The simplicity of Christ means we adhere to one ultimate influence. When our minds are opened to the powerful, virtually hypnotic influence of the devil, we are as unstable as a staggering drunk. Just as it requires a little time for other kinds of toxins to be washed out of our systems, it takes a little time for the poison the evil one has poured into our minds to drain. We do wake up, however, and, boy, are we mad.

I don't know the core of these druglike feelings many people describe, but I wonder if it has something to do with the Greek word *pharmakeia,* which is translated "witchcraft" (Gal. 5:20). Most believers recognize illicit drug use as an overpowering seduction of the devil, but I wonder if Satan can somehow "drug" the mind through steady and increasing doses of subtle deception. I don't have the answer. I'm not sure we can be biblically dogmatic about how far God allows Satan to go in his dealings with a believer, but we can know that he's going as far as he can. Scripture emphatically teaches that we can be beguiled. Sounds a little mind altering to me.

Right about now the righteous legalists are probably having a fit, thinking, *Woman, you've just supplied flagrant sinners with a "devil-made-me-do-it" excuse for rebellion.* God forbid. In fact, if the victims—temporarily turned ungodly—do not take full responsibility for their sin, they cannot find freedom and restoration. Keep in mind that we never have to do God's job. He always knows the truth, and eventually so does every believer who commits acts of ungodliness. Each one of us is wise to "commune with your own heart upon your bed, and be silent" (Ps. 4:4 AMP). In other words, we must each search our own heart and approach God in complete honesty. We would never be wise to lie to the Holy Spirit, who knows the motivation for every action. Thankfully, both the sins we commit in reaction to seduction and those we commit in outright rebellion can be forgiven through the payment Christ has made for *all* sins on the cross. However, we must approach the throne of grace *with* truth and *in* truth.

16. Feelings of devastation and indescribable sorrow finally came, ushering in deep repentance.

This point is critical as we specify the focus of our case study. Nominal or halfhearted Christians may come out of a season of defeat without excessive sorrow, but those who were *wholeheartedly, sincerely, and purely devoted to Christ* (2 Cor. 11:3 AMP) finally experience such a devastation that they often feel they can't go on. The entire third portion of this book deals with repentance and restoration.

Right about now, some readers feel like someone's been reading their mail. You know all too well exactly what I've just described. But how about all the other readers? Are you still with me? Please hang in there with me until the end of the book, even if this chapter seemed far-fetched for you. I'm really not a wigged-out left-winger. I am a Baptist, for crying out loud! I still love old hymns and give to foreign missions. I still believe many things that fall between the traditional boundaries. I will readily admit to you that "we" ordinarily don't even believe in stuff like this, and I'm not sure right this minute that "they" want to claim me.

My dilemma is that I've seen too much, experienced too much, and studied too much to totally discount what completely unrelated and perfectly lucid people are saying. Satan doesn't appear to be acting like a good Baptist believes he should. I'm mad about it, too, but I broke free from denial too long ago to act like there's no trouble in River City. I may be thinking outside the lines of my usual belief system, but, for the life of me, I do not believe I am thinking outside the lines of God's Word. This I know: God would not let me rest until I told what I've seen. I have never been more certain He sent me forth with a message. I will trust Him with it.

I think I can assure you that this chapter is the only one that tips the scale into the realm of the experiential. From this point on, I can substantiate every point I will make with solid Scripture. Why don't you come with me and see? Surely you're curious to know how a godly person could be vulnerable to the kind of mess we just described. That's next, so you'd better stay tuned.

SUSCEPTIBLE TO SEDUCTION

We've arrived at a very important place. At the end of our previous chapter, I promised we would discuss how a *wholeheartedly, sincerely,* and *purely devoted* servant of Jesus Christ could become vulnerable to such powerfully demonic seduction. If you're thinking, *Surely there is* something *that the enemy is latching onto,* you are absolutely right.

You might be tempted to say, "Aha! See there! I knew they were not innocent!" Oh, beloved, I never said they . . . or *we* . . . were *innocent.* No believer is ever forced into a sinful season. At the same time I will tell you that the thing Satan latches onto often is not *sin.*

Remember, we're talking about godly people with wholehearted devotion who were seduced. None of us is ever sinless, but these people were not living under the *dominion* of any sin when they were attacked. No, sin is not where the enemy most often gets his foothold on the godly. Rather, we're about to see, where this kind of victim is concerned, the enemy more often latches on to weakness—or maybe I should say a hidden spot of vulnerability. Of course, Satan knows that weakness can turn to sin in a heartbeat when exposed to just the right amount of pressure.

> In his arrogance the wicked man hunts down the
>   weak,
> who are caught in the schemes he devises.
>   (Ps. 10:2)

After the case studies I've encountered in the last several years, I have become more and more convinced that victims of seduction share certain vulnerabilities at the time of their attack. Again, I can't imagine that my list includes all points of susceptibility, so be assured up front that I'm far from knowing it all. Furthermore, please do not assume you haven't been seduced if every shoe doesn't fit.

At this point, let me identify for you the most important person reading this chapter: the one who has never been seduced but shares these vulnerabilities. Child of God, be warned! You are susceptible to the nightmare of your life! Devour part 2 of this book before the lion devours you!

Here is my list of the weaknesses that many Christians carry in their hearts, minds, and souls. Please consider them carefully.

1. Ignorance.

Without exception, the number one element that sets believers up for seduction is ignorance! I tried to think of a prettier word, but this is the one the Bible uses. Don't think I mean this as one of my colloquialisms. I am using it in its most literal sense. What we do not know *can hurt us!*

Throughout the remainder of the list, you will see signs of ignorance—things the seduced did not know. Obviously one of the most common forms of ignorance was that none of them *knew* this kind of thing could happen. Meditate on the following Scriptures:

- Speaking of the high priests that served in the Old Testament tabernacle, the writer of Hebrews said, "He is able to deal gently with those who are ignorant and are going astray, since he himself is subject to weakness" (Heb. 5:2). Note the kinds of persons receiving the ministry. Don't miss the words *ignorant, going astray,* and *weakness.* We are at great risk of going astray over ignorance and weakness.

- In the Amplified Bible, 2 Corinthians 2:11 tells us to forgive, "to keep Satan from getting the advantage over us; for we are not ignorant of his wiles and intentions." The apostle Paul and his well-educated crew may not have been ignorant of Satan's schemes, but most of us are! We cannot afford such ignorance, particularly as the "Day is drawing near"! We cannot ignore him and assume he'll go away. Ignorance flies like a flag over our heads screaming, "Pick me! Pick me!"

- Five times in his epistles, the apostle Paul repeated, "I would not have you ignorant." I can't help sharing these last two Scriptures because I have looked back on my times of defeat and cried bitter, angry tears with my own rendition of these verses. Psalm 73:22 declares, "So foolish was I, and ignorant: I was as a beast before thee" (KJV). Then Agur confessed, "I am the most ignorant of men; I do not have a man's understanding, I have not learned wisdom, nor have I knowledge of the Holy One" (Prov. 30:2–3).

How many times have I looked at some of the ways I allowed Satan to defeat me in the past and cried to myself, "How could you be so stupid! You idiot! Haven't you learned *anything*?" One of the things God has had to work diligently on in my life is my own self-condemnation. Long after I was set free, I was still punishing myself unmercifully. So much so, it became its own form of bondage. God has really had to deal with me on this issue.

The last thing I want to do is give the enemy I have come to hate with such a perfect hatred another moment's satisfaction; that's exactly what self-condemnation does. Let's be delivered. Our next point will unfold the area of ignorance that drains our strength faster than any other.

2. Spiritual passion that exceeds biblical knowledge.

Let's return once again to our focal Scripture and read it carefully with this point in mind: "But [now] I am fearful lest that even as the serpent beguiled Eve by his cunning, so your minds may be corrupted and seduced from wholehearted and sincere and pure devotion to Christ" (2 Cor. 11:3 AMP). Notice that the Scripture talks about the serpent getting to our hearts through our minds. The person described in this Scripture has wholehearted devotion to Christ, but the mind still vulnerable. Most of ours are too—until we have a horrible scare that teaches us to love God with our whole mind and not just our whole heart. The church in Corinth was passionate but lacked the knowledge to provide a firm, less shakable foundation.

In our previous chapter, we highlighted Paul's brief thesis on tearing down strongholds: "Casting down imaginations, and every high thing that exalteth itself against the knowledge of God" (2 Cor. 10:5 KJV). If we don't have the knowledge of God, we are ill-equipped to recognize imaginations that are exalting themselves over God. In essence, that's exactly what the writer of Proverbs 30:2–3 was saying:

> I am the most ignorant of men;
>> I do not have a man's understanding.
> I have not learned wisdom.
>> nor have I knowledge of the Holy One.

We can't just have knowledge about warfare to defeat Satan. We desperately need the knowledge of God, the knowledge of the Holy One! Our only means of getting it is through an intense relationship with God through His Word. Mind you, I would have told you I had a pretty fair knowledge of Scripture at times of defeat, but in retrospect I knew bits and pieces rather than grasping more of the whole counsel of God. Furthermore, a big difference exists between a head full of knowledge and the words of God literally abiding in us.

Had we not read Jessie's story in the second chapter, someone might want to ask, "Why do so many godly pastors fall to the seduction of Satan when they are constantly preparing sermons?" Please allow me to speak to those dear brothers who have been so devastated. Many of them unknowingly fell into the trap of spending time in the Word almost entirely for message preparation. That, of course, was Satan's first goal.

Satan strongly desires the destruction of anyone who keeps his or her sword of the Spirit (the Word of God) sharpened by personal use. He knows that weapon becomes dull once the believer's use of Scripture becomes mechanical. Many of those in ministry who fell for seduction had gotten so busy doing the work of God that they slipped away from pure intimacy with God.

All of us who have been called to communicate to the Body of Christ must be radically cautious to remember that God doesn't just want to talk *through* us. He wants to talk *to* us. Intimately. Sometimes in ways that are none of anyone else's business. When we cease letting God speak to us, it is only a matter of time before He will cease speaking through us.

Before we move on to the next point, please allow me to offer a word of caution on the other side of this double-edged issue. Yes, spiritual passion exceeding biblical knowledge is a definite weakness, and so is the opposite condition. Please beware! A head full of biblical knowledge without a heart passionately in love with Christ is terribly dangerous—a stronghold waiting to happen. The head is full, but the heart and soul are still unsatisfied. Satan knows that we all long for passion. If we are not given to godly passion, we will be tempted by counterfeits.

Completely passionate and biblically knowledgeable! *Oh, God, make us both!*

3. A lack of discernment.

I am convinced that discernment will be one of the most important criteria in the devoted believer's life to provide protection from seduction. Most victims of seduction have not had a history of particularly great discernment. Glance at the following Scriptures and relate them to our subject matter:

- Proverbs 14:33: "Wisdom reposes in the heart of the discerning / and even among fools she lets herself be known." Wisdom discerns when she's around fools!
- Proverbs 28:11: "A rich man may be wise in his own eyes, / but a poor man who has discernment sees through him." Do you see? A discerning man can see through some of the lies others even tell themselves!
- Proverbs 19:25: "Rebuke a discerning man, and he will gain knowledge." Beloved, do you see that those who have discernment don't get defensive and start rationalizing when they're rebuked! Instead, they gain knowledge. Hallelujah!
- Philippians 1:9–10: "This is my prayer: that your love may abound more and more in knowledge and depth of insight, so that you may be able to discern what is best and may be pure and blameless until the day of Christ."

I so desperately want to be pure and blameless. After God finally got through to me and broke my cycle of defeat, I began praying with all my might, "God, I can't do anything to change the past. I have been neither pure nor blameless, but would You enable me by the power of Your Word and through the filling of Your Holy Spirit to live every day of my remaining years in purity? As a virgin bride?" Oh, beloved, I want it so badly, I can hardly bear it. To come anywhere close to my deep hope, I am going to need lots of discernment.

I could list many other biblical proofs, but I think you can see my point. Discernment is critical. Do you see how susceptible any of us can be to seduction without it? Celebrate the fact that God honors the heartfelt petition for discernment and will graciously give it and more. Do you remember Solomon's petition? "So give your servant a discerning heart to govern your people and to distinguish between right and wrong. . . . The Lord was pleased that Solomon asked for this. So God said to him . . . I will do what you have asked. I will give you a wise and discerning heart, . . . Moreover, I will give you what you have not asked for" (1 Kings 3:9–13).

Don't miss the fact that Solomon was already wise enough to know that sometimes right and wrong can be hard to distinguish. He needed discernment and so do we. In our next point, we're going to find out that we need a kind of discernment we don't often consider.

4. A lack of self-discernment.

This one is so important! We'll let David, a man who certainly fell into sin after godliness, introduce it to us through his very private prayer. He wrote:

> Who can discern his errors?
>   Forgive my hidden faults.
>   Keep your servant also from willful sins;
>   may they not rule over me.
>   Then will I be blameless,
>   innocent of great transgression. (Ps. 19:12–13)

I can go no further without writing on paper what I've just said aloud to God. Oh, I love God's Word. Isn't it rich? He has all the answers! He knows what we need! Nothing in this world is more exciting to me than doing what you and I are doing this moment: digging through God's Word together. I just love it.

Were you as blown away by the question in Psalm 19:12 as I was? I memorized this psalm years ago but didn't catch the importance of it until recently when I taught it in Sunday school! "Who can discern his errors?" Who is David talking about? Himself! Grab a Bible and look at the context. Each of the final three verses in Psalm 19 concern the writer himself and his deep desire for God to help him personally. He desires that God be pleased with what He sees deep within.

In this particular verse, the Hebrew word translated "error" is *segihah*. According to the Old Testament Lexical Aids of the *Key Study Bible*, it means "error, transgression, sin committed inadvertently."[1] It stands in contrast to the psalmist's petition for God to keep him also from willful sins. We commit some sins willfully and presumptuously. We commit others inadvertently. The former flows from rebellion and the latter from error, ignorance, and weakness. Again, it's all sin, but we need to distinguish that rebellion is not the only way to get into trouble.

The word *segihah* comes from the word *sagah*. Hang on to your hat while I tell you what this word means in all its different applications. I'm going to write it word for word as it appears in these Old Testament Lexical Aids: "Sagah: to waver, wander, go astray (Eze 34:6); to lead astray (Job 12:16), misdirect (the blind [Dt 27:18]), seduce; to sin through ignorance, transgress inadvertently (1 Sa 26:21); to reel (as if intoxicated [Pr 20:1; Isa 28:7]). Evil habits (Pr 20:1; Isa 28:7), immorality (Pr 5:20), and spiritual weakness (Pr 19:27) cause individuals to stray from God's commands (Ps 119:21, 118), much like sheep gradually stray from their shepherd (Eze 34:6). Sagah is also used with reference to a man intoxicated with love (Pr 5:19, 20)."[2]

A couple of things are of great interest to me here. Keep in mind that the original word for *errors* in Psalm 19:12 comes from this word. These definitions show the close relationship between ignorance, spiritual weakness, and going astray. I also find the references to "reel (as if intoxicated)" and "intoxicated with love" very interesting in terms of our previous chapter. More than anything, I hope you didn't miss the sudden appearance of the word *seduce*. I believe the implication could be twofold:

- First, our weaknesses and areas of ignorance are huge vulnerabilities to seduction, which can quickly lead to sins committed inadvertently.
- I see a second possible implication as well. We know for a fact that Satan's seduction is purposeful and scheming and is utterly intended for evil. It is well planned and timed, and nothing about it is accidental or coincidental. In cases where this applies, are the mortals he chooses to use as the agents of seduction always evil, malicious, and completely intentional?

Let's see what Scripture implies on the subject. According to Scripture, mortal agents can fall into several different categories.

One is found in 1 Timothy 4:1–2: "The Spirit clearly says that in later times some will abandon the faith and follow deceiving spirits and things taught by demons. Such teachings come through hypocritical liars, whose consciences have been seared as with a hot iron." A pretty scathing indictment against those who are such willing servants of Satan's seductions.

Second Timothy 3:1–7 also addresses those who can be powerfully used by the enemy to seduce other lives. You'll notice in this reference that the target is not described with *wholehearted, pure, sincere devotion.* Rather, this object of strongly implicated seduction is loaded down with sins. Needless to say, anytime we are *loaded down with sins,* we are game for seduction.

> But mark this: There will be terrible times in the last days. People will be lovers of themselves, lovers of money, boastful, proud, abusive, disobedient to their parents, ungrateful, unholy, without love, unforgiving, slanderous, without self-control, brutal, not lovers of the good, treacherous, rash, conceited, lovers of pleasure rather than lovers of God—having a form of godliness but denying its power. Have nothing to do with them. They are the kind who worm their way into homes and gain control over weak-willed women, who are loaded down with sins and are swayed by all kinds of evil desires, always learning but never able to acknowledge the truth. (2 Tim. 3:1–7)

Another scathing indictment against those who worm their ways into the lives of others. Furthermore, most of the seducers and seductresses mentioned in Proverbs were intentional in their actions. Most, but not all. Look back at the definition of *sagah* one more time. Part of the definition read: "seduce; to sin through ignorance, transgress inadvertently." Could it be that some who are used as puppets or agents for Satan's seductions did not willfully and presumptuously volunteer for the job? Could it be that sometimes Satan's mortal agents of seduction have themselves been seduced? I think so. In fact, the seduced may become seducers if they fail to let God radically deal with them through and through.

I've been asked if I think two people caught in relational seduction can *both* be taken by surprise, neither being a more willing agent. While I have no intention of becoming the Ann Landers of seductive relationships, the possibility seems reasonable. Remember, the *lawlessness* of Satan's work is *secretive* (2 Thess. 2:7). We won't be able to figure out every detail, but if we'll learn what we can, we'll be protected from what we can't.

We are vastly helped when we recognize our own errors, our own transgressions, and the ways in which we've committed sins inadvertently. We are so quick to acknowledge the errors of others, but one of our best defenses is to recognize where we've each gone wrong and where our own personal weak places are. We've got to replace our *self-condemnation* with *self-discernment!* Lord, help us!

Next, I want you to examine another cause of vulnerability. We need to deal with weaknesses caused by:

5. Exposure to or experience with false worship or depravity in the past.

I am convinced that one reason the apostle Paul was so worried about the Corinthian church is because they had been exposed to so much false worship and depravity. Indeed, many of them had come directly from those practices. They had fallen for such false teaching in the past that he feared they could be "had" again: "you put up with it easily enough" (2 Cor. 11:4). Not only that, they were still surrounded by ungodliness in their attempts to live godly lives.

Corinth was a vile city even by our standards today. Not unlike us, they were constantly exposed to the worship of false idols, sexual looseness, and nudity. Where their exposure was literal (right in the middle of the street or on the temple grounds as perverted "worship"), in this country ours is often through billboards, covers of magazines at the grocery story, television shows, and perhaps even worse, commercials! Of course the seeker of pornography could tap into endless resources, but we don't have to go nearly that far to be susceptible to seduction.

Any level of *overexposure* can open a door in the mind that Satan might one day decide to take for his advantage. Some of us were exposed to things we should never have seen as children. We don't have to want to be exposed to be exposed. For instance, being exposed to pornography can take a profound toll on the later life, and Satan often makes sure it does. I've heard people talk about finding pornographic magazines in their father's things when they were young, then dismiss it as unimportant. Such a discovery frequently has a huge effect on that life and gives Satan a trump card for later.

Needless to say, *experience can open an even wider door than exposure.* Satan would be a fool not to try to exploit our past experiences. How many people have come to salvation in Jesus Christ and been forgiven and made new only for Satan to continue to taunt them, accuse them, remind them, and tempt them with past memories of sinful activities? God keeps no record of wrongs, but you can bet Satan does. He's a meticulous note taker. We've got to start believing God's press about us and not the devil's.

We have such unbelief concerning our new identities in Christ that we practically let Satan get away with murder—the murder of a new self-concept defined in the Word of God.

I want to share a part of my personal testimony so someone might realize how Satan can use our pasts against us. Although I have committed plenty of willful sin in my life, weaknesses left from my childhood became the most powerful "trump card" Satan was able to use against me. As far too young a child, I not only was exposed to things I shouldn't have been, but I was forced to experience some things no child should ever experience. As I grew up, I tucked many of those memories as far down in my subconscious as possible. If my mind tried to pull them up, I would stuff them back down. The problem was, Satan had stuffed them in his pocket for later. I can hardly keep from getting red in the face with anger as I tell you that he waited for just the right circumstances to flood my life with a tidal wave of attack. In addition to my victimization, I had also made numerous poor choices. Don't think he didn't use those against me as well.

We have raised the question, "Can anyone be seduced?" I still maintain that while it is possible, there are those for whom it is highly *improbable.* I have the privilege of writing for the same discipleship publishing house as Dr. Henry Blackaby and T. W. Hunt, two men whose shoes I don't consider myself worthy to shine. We know that Satan despises any teacher who dares to instruct believers how to use the Sword of the Spirit. He would do anything he could to destroy any of us. If Satan were to survey Dr. Blackaby, Dr. Hunt, and Beth Moore, looking for someone to seduce, who would be his more susceptible or vulnerable candidate? Hands down, someone more like *me!* Both of those fine men have led pure lives with very little *exposure to* or *experience with* wickedness. They have long track records of faithfulness. Thankfully, by the time I started writing alongside those two fine men, God had taught me volumes, and I was no longer easy prey. I've even learned how to punch the devil back. Still, I will always have to be on guard because I have a past other less-vulnerable believers don't have.

Dear one, if we don't let God deal with every part of our pasts, our hurts, our secrets, our errors in judgment, our mistakes, our sins, or the handicaps in our backgrounds, any one of them can be like a hibernating bear. Satan, the prowling lion, stalks the mouth of the cave, waiting for just the "right" season. He opens his jaws and lets out a roar so ferocious that the heavens tremble. Only mortals cannot hear the lion roar. The bear stirs. The roars continue. The bear resurrects from its death-like slumber, rises to its feet, and realizes he is ravenous. The lion hides and watches while the bear eats you alive. I've heard the stories so many times:

"So what if I was molested as a child. It's never bothered me before."

"I never knew my father. He bailed on us and ran off with a seventeen-year-old when I was three years old. I don't care. I never give the lousy excuse-for-a-man a second thought."

"My mom was in an asylum for most of my young life. Mentally ill. I just feel sorry for her, that's all."

"My mom had me dancing in a topless joint for money when I was still a minor. Some kind of mom, huh? I just try never to think about it."

"I watched my father beat my mother nearly to death. He was the meanest drunk you can imagine. I'm never gonna be like him. In fact, I don't even think I'll ever get married."

"My dad was a pastor. We used to have to sit on the front row every Sunday and listen to him bang the pulpit, condemning the congregation for their horrible sins. You should have seen him at home. He made me sick."

"My sister died of cancer when she was nine and I was five. Our family never got over it. I don't remember a single sound of laughter in our house."

"My brother and I were in a fire when we were little boys. He burned to death. I've still got scars, but I go on living. You just can't let those kinds of things get to you."

Not a single one of these examples or any in our wildest imagination is beyond God's awesome ability to diffuse. And we would know if He has diffused them or not because He wisely requires a little cooperation and honesty on our part. If left with a fuse, however, we're not unlike Cain when he refused to bring to the altar what he knew God wanted. "Sin is crouching at your door; it desires to have you, but you must master it" (Gen. 4:7). We bring God a few obligatory sheaves when what He wants is the animal that could destroy us.

Beloved, listen to me carefully. Satan plays hardball. The psalmist testified about his foes and his powerful enemy with the words, "They confronted me in the day of my disaster" (Ps. 18:18). Somehow we secretly hope the devil, as low as he is, surely has enough scruples to draw the line where the fight would be totally unfair. *Satan has no scruples!* When we have a disaster, we can count on him being right there confronting us at our weakest, most vulnerable point. Would he take advantage of a helpless child? *Yes!* Would he descend on the life of a grieving mother? *Without question!* Would he capitalize on a past we've tried so hard to put behind us? *Count on it!* We can't just put our pasts behind us. We've got to put our pasts *in front of God.* Satan is inconceivably mean and will take advantage of any unfinished business.

In his book *The Ragamuffin Gospel,* Brennan Manning wrote,

> Often I have been asked, "Brennan, how is it
> possible that you became an alcoholic after you
> got saved?" It is possible because I got battered and
> bruised by loneliness and failure, because I got

discouraged, uncertain, guilt-ridden, and took my
eyes off Jesus.[3]

In his later work *Ruthless Trust,* he adds this insight to his
testimony:

> The biggest obstacle on my journey of trust
> has been an oppressive sense of insecurity, inade-
> quacy, inferiority, and low self-esteem. I have no
> memory of being held, hugged, or kissed by my
> mother as a little boy. I was called a nuisance and a
> pest and told to shut up and be still. My mother
> had been orphaned at age three—both her parents
> died in a flu epidemic in Montreal—and sent to
> an orphanage where she lived for several years,
> until she was eventually adopted. Then, at age
> eighteen, she moved to Brooklyn, New York, for
> training as a registered nurse. Having received little
> attention or affection through those early years,
> she was incapable of giving any.[4]

Surely we don't think for a moment that after this man
received Christ as his Savior then surrendered his life to ministry,
Satan didn't use the unfinished business of his past to destroy his
hell-threatening future. The Body of Christ is blessed indeed—
not only that Satan didn't get away with his full scheme—but that
God allowed him to get away with a portion of it so Manning
would minister to us out of his wealth of experience. What God
has used Manning to bring to the mixed bag of our generation of

believers may be a gift without parallel. God has brought much glory through his sufferings and, no doubt, much of his sufferings stemmed from Satan's relentless manipulation of his past.

If you're like I used to be, you might be in a pout about now, thinking, *But it's not fair that my past makes me more vulnerable! We can't do anything about our pasts!* Oh, beloved, if that last statement is not one of the deadliest doctrines of demons, I don't know what is! Don't you see? The very thing Satan used against me was precisely that I had not done anything about my past! Yes, we can do something about our pasts. We can take them to Jesus! We can't forget them or ignore them. We need Him to take full authority over them where they are no longer a playground for the enemy. Jesus is our Alpha and our Omega. He has been there from our "beginning" and will be faithful to us until the "end." He longs to reframe our pasts and let us see them against the backdrop of His glory. Never ever forget that our God is a redeemer. Celebrate the song of ascent in Psalm 130:3–4, 7:

> If you, O LORD, kept a record of sins,
>> O Lord, who could stand?
> But with you there is forgiveness;
>> therefore you are feared.
>
> . . . .
>
> O Israel, put your hope in the LORD,
>> for with the LORD is unfailing love
>> and with him is *full redemption.* (emphasis mine)

Dear one, let Him redeem it! Every bit of your past! Not just the injustices but the blatant sins. Not just the accidental ones but the willful ones! And not just our sins, but our excruciating losses. For thirty years Satan used my past in various ways. I finally began to wake up to the fact that Satan was going to use my past until I allowed God to snatch it from him and *use it for Himself!* No, I don't have to go parading it and sharing the graphics of it. I've just learned to give God full authority over it and bring every part of my past under His wings. Into His possession. I have given Him permission to take every one of my memories captive to Christ, and now I can no longer see my abuses and sins in their own accord or in the hands of Satan. Now I see them in the healing, forgiving, nail-scarred hands of Jesus where He is cleansing them and transforming them into the stuff of mercy. Now, instead of Satan using them periodically as he did in the past, God uses them every single day! In ministry. In parenting. In friendships. Oh, beloved, let Him have it! He is so trustworthy!

God never abuses His authority. He also never shames. Do you remember the woman at the well? After her encounter with Jesus, she ran into town saying, "He told me everything I ever did!" (John 4:39). And she wasn't ashamed! Do you know why? Because when Christ takes authority over our pasts and we allow Him to confront them, treat them, and heal them, we exchange our shame for dignity! I'm ready to shout hallelujah!

At the beginning of this chapter, we discussed that when Satan targets a believer who has *wholehearted, sincere, and pure devotion to Christ,* he latches on to weakness more often than sin. You may be wondering, "But what about the sins of our pasts?" Beloved, one of the times when Satan pounced on me most ferociously and used my past sins against me, I had already repented of those sins. They could no longer be used as "sins" against me. But here's the catch: they were still weaknesses! Why? Because I had asked God to forgive me, but I had never asked God to heal me completely, redeem my past, restore my life, sanctify me entirely, and help me to forgive myself. Until I allowed God to take full authority over them in every way, my past sins—though turned from and forgiven—were still vulnerabilities where Satan could prey. Thank goodness, they're not anymore, and yours don't have to be either. Is this speaking to you right now? Have you been any of the places I've described? God is so inconceivably faithful. He has not done a single thing for me that He is not ready and anxious to do for you. Hear His tender voice speak to you now. "Take courage! It is I. Don't be afraid."

Trust Him! With every inch of your past, present, and future. Because until you do, you are susceptible to seduction.

CHAPTER 5

GOD'S
PERMISSIVE WILL

W hy in the world would God allow someone with *whole-hearted and sincere and pure devotion to Christ* to get caught in the snare of demonic seduction? Even the less mature believer can make sense of the fact that God develops strength in His children through various trials and tribulations, but *demonic seduction?* What purpose could it possibly serve? After all, it doesn't even seem fair, does it?

You see, we're not talking about your usual brand of temptation when we're addressing the seduction of the saints. Daily we have all sorts of challenges and temptations, some a little more intense than others, but under average conditions many godly people walk steadfastly for the duration without much of a hitch. Not in perfection, of course. But in *victory*.

What we're talking about in this book is something many believers have not experienced. *Yet*, that is. Perhaps they never will. Wouldn't that be nice? It sure would, but I wouldn't put all my eggs in that happy basket. Not considering the generation we are living in. Anyone with a hint of spiritual discernment can feel the heat rising. I think we'd better do everything we can to fortify ourselves in case we get targeted.

The difference between our everyday temptations and a pointed, intentionally destructive demonic seduction is the difference between a snowball and an avalanche. We can see the added intensification in varying seasons of attack even in the earthly life of Christ. He no doubt had temptations on an ongoing basis but perhaps nothing compared to the full-scale season of temptation in the wilderness.

I heard a testimony recently about a dear pastor in his early sixties who had walked with God uprightly all his believing life. Although he had amazing compassion for a man who had never really experienced failure, he had no reference point for understanding how Christian people could get into some of the messes he had counseled. He was a very godly man and was neither boastful of his good track record nor judgmental of others who were slightly muddier. In the inmost places of his heart and mind, he simply did not understand.

When this pastor reached his late fifties, something totally unexpected happened. A season of darkness fell upon him: an indescribable heaviness of spirit that neither he nor others could tie to anything circumstantial or physiological. As if the darkness and depression were not enough to cope with, he then began to struggle with lustful, truly pornographic thoughts unlike anything he had ever experienced. Even his teen years had presented him with nothing like the temptations he faced with total astonishment in his late fifties. He was literally bombarded with evil thoughts.

Praise God, he endured the months of suffering and temptation without physically committing adultery, but he did temporarily succumb to uncharacteristic behavior, and those around him were not unaffected. As the season ended, he was personally devastated and found himself asking the question so many others have asked: "What was that?" That, dear brothers and sisters in Christ, was seduction. If my hunch is right, things of this nature will only increase in number, which is why we must be warned and fortified.

As we reflect on our previous chapter, what makes this pastor's situation fairly frightening is that I'm unaware of any of the four areas of susceptibility. That's one reason I want to make clear that those who aren't among the high-risk believers are still not immune. No doubt, this man's low-risk profile guarded him against more grievous trespasses in his season of temptation, but it did not keep him from being bombarded.

Thankfully, this precious man of God has experienced the tender mercies of Jehovah Rapha, and he actively serves God, as he should. Our question in this chapter, however, is why would God allow a man of his character to be assaulted by the evil one in the manner that he was? Although Ephesians 6 does not tell us *why*, it certainly alerts us to the reality of a dangerous enemy and a furious war. No matter how many times you have read the following Scriptures, I ask you to read them again slowly and reflectively, not giving way to the rubber flesh of familiarity.

In conclusion, be strong in the Lord—be empowered through your union with Him; draw

your strength from Him—that strength which
His [boundless] might provides. Put on God's
whole armor—the armor of a heavy-armed sol-
dier, which God supplies—that you may be able
successfully to stand up against [all] the strategies
and the deceits of the devil. For we are not
wrestling with flesh and blood—contending only
with physical opponents—but against the despo-
tisms, against the powers, against [the master
spirits who are] the world rulers of this present
darkness, against the spirit forces of wickedness
in the heavenly (supernatural) sphere. Therefore
put on God's complete armor, that you may be
able to resist and stand your ground on the evil
day [of danger], and having done all [the crisis
demands], to stand [firmly in your place].
(Eph. 6:10–13 AMP)

Where the Amplified Bible uses the words "strategies and the
deceits of the devil," the KJV uses the words "wiles of the devil."
The NIV and the NASB both employ the word *schemes*. Whether
translated "strategies," "wiles," or "schemes," these come from the
Greek word *methodeia*. Below are several different definitions
offered by various translation experts. Take a moment to meditate
on the magnitude of what they are suggesting.

- "The word means: Schemes, wiles, strategies and tricks; trickery. It means the deceits, craftiness, trickery, methods, and
  strategies which the devil uses to wage war against the

believer. Practical Application: The enemy is the devil. . . . He will do everything he can to deceive and capture the believer.[1]

- "[comp. 'method']; travelling over, i.e. travesty (trickery): — wile, lie in wait."[2]
- "Method, the following or pursuing of an orderly and technical procedure in the handling of a subject."[3]

No matter how often I've seen or even shared the definitions of *methodeia,* my skin crawls every time. I hope you absorbed the concept soberly. The most obvious English word found in the Greek is *method.* If we could only understand that the devil does not work haphazardly but carefully, methodically, weaving and spinning, and watching for just the right time. He truly has method to his madness. He draws out plans and executes them very carefully. He carefully sets traps for the express purpose of wreaking destruction in the lives of the saints.

Earlier we discussed that anything God does, Satan attempts to counterfeit. One of the first biblical principles most believers learn concerning their new agenda is that God has a *plan* for their lives. Please hear this with your whole heart, believer: *so does Satan.* Consider the following truths and their suggested counterfeits:

- "For I know the plans I have for you," declares the LORD, "plans to prosper you and not to harm you, plans to give you hope and a future" (Jer. 29:11).
- "For I know the plans I have for you," declares the devil, "plans to totally bankrupt you and to harm you, plans to make you hopeless and to destroy your future."

Somehow in the life of the dear brother I mentioned earlier, Satan had devised a scheme toward the probable and general goal I just suggested. To the glory of God, Satan didn't destroy the pastor's future, but he certainly played havoc on that "present" season. The late fifties may have seemed untimely to the pastor, but it was the perfect time to the enemy. Often our times of assault will come when we're least expecting them. But why does God allow them at all? Since God's ways are so much higher than ours and His thoughts so far beyond us, we won't wholly be able to answer this question. God has ordained that a certain amount of mystery shrouds the full understanding of His sovereignty. Put in simple language, we simply do not have the tools to understand God. We will, however, discover some answers that *are* available to us.

First, let's be perfectly clear from the beginning that God never appoints us to sin. Even when He tests His children, His purpose is to prove godly character . . . or perhaps the lack thereof. If a test proves a lack, God's chief desire is to enlist the cooperation of the child and provide what is lacking. God *never* tempts us to sin, nor does He ever fail to provide a way of escape, just as He promised in 1 Corinthians 10:13. Scripture is clear that we are tempted through two sources: (1) the devil, also called the tempter (1 Thess. 3:5) and (2) our own lusts (James 1:14). Needless to say, they work most effectively in tandem, which is why Satan does everything he can to awaken the lusts of his target.

Both Old and New Testament Scripture support the idea that Satan has to gain God's permission to wage an all-out war upon one of His redeemed. Job 1 is a perfect Old Testament example.

Do you know that many scholars believe the Book of Job is one of the oldest books of the Bible? I find that very significant since it concerns a man, His God, and an unseen war.

You might take a fresh look at Job. The older I get, the more unsettling it seems. Do you realize Job endured the entire excruciating ordeal without ever knowing he was in the middle of a match between the God of the universe and the head dragon of hell? Even at the conclusion of the Old Testament book, Job still had no idea. He had learned plenty about the sovereignty of God, but he still had no concept of the faith God had shown in him. Don't you think Job would have had an easier time if God had said, "Listen, son. I know this is horribly painful, but something much bigger than you know is at stake here. You are a truly righteous man in an unrighteous world. Satan thinks you'll crumble if I draw back some of your protection and blessing. I want him to see that you won't. So, as hard as this is, you stand firm! All the hosts of heaven are rooting for you, and all the unholy hosts of hell are jeering at you. Win a big one for the team, won't you?"

That kind of explanation would have made a tremendous difference to me. What about you? What could be more motivating than a fierce spirit of competition? Right this minute, I'm picturing a replay of the climactic last scene of the movie *Rudy*. All the main character ever wanted to do was play football for Notre Dame. He gets accepted to the school but isn't good enough for the team. Finally they let him attend practice. Before long the other players see that he has spunk even if he lacks size. It's the last game of his senior year, and he finally gets to suit up. The game is almost over. The teammates are watching the clock, hoping the coach will put him in the game. Suddenly the team and the fans begin cheering, "Rudy! Rudy! Rudy!" It's the last play of the game. The coach sends him out on the field, and the little runt in a big Notre Dame football uniform runs with every ounce of energy he has across the field while his daddy cheers in the stands.

Keith and I bawl our eyes out every single time we watch that movie, sitting transfixed until the credits roll. Our favorite part is when the words come on the screen saying that no one else has ever been carried off the football field by a Notre Dame team. Nope, not one. Just *Rudy*. If I keep thinking about it, I may have to bawl again. We and countless other Americans have watched that silly movie over and over. Why? Oh, go ahead and admit it, you proud oaf. We all want to be a Rudy! Wouldn't that be the ultimate?

If we knew the stakes were high and we were in the middle of a paramount competition, we would throw everything we had into it, wouldn't we? The fact is, *we are in such a competition.* We just don't realize it. Neither did Job. I have wondered over and over what his face looked like when he got to heaven and they told him what was going on in the unseen world while he was down below. Surely God still has that scene on videotape because I want to check it out and watch it one heavenly day.

Don't you know Job was so thankful he had chosen to believe God and remain faithful? Can you imagine how strange Job must have felt to realize *he* had been chosen by God to fight one of the hardest earthly battles in history? In humanly inexplicable ways, God allowed Job to be tested so harshly because He, *God,* had faith in him, *Job.* Amazing.

We're not out of our reach doctrinally to assume that the same huge competition in the heavenlies takes place all around us. That's exactly what Ephesians 6:10–12 says. Who's to say when things really get tough that we, and countless other believers, have not momentarily been chosen to prove faithful to God? You and I have no idea what's going on in the unseen world when we're being attacked. If we were in the middle of that kind of competition, wouldn't we want to *win?* I love knowing God's team is always going to win, but I want to be part of the victory *myself.* Rudy's team had won lots of games, but plenty of teammates had blown their plays.

When Satan turns up the heat, I often say something like this to myself: *You have no idea what's going on out there, old girl. This could be really important. Stand firm and don't give the yell leaders of hell anything to cheer about. God is for you.* Back up a second. Do you realize God is *for you?* Yes, the stakes are high. Yes, the battle is rough and sometimes seems unbearable, but *God is always for us.* Then why does He let our opponents hit us so hard? To prove that we, mere mortal flesh and blood, terribly self-centered by nature, really are *for God.*

Perhaps right about now, you're feeling sick inside thinking, *But I've already blown my play. I failed my test.* Listen here, brother or sister. Do you want to talk about someone who has blown some plays? I have! But I'm thankful to say God didn't take me off the team. He took me to the locker room, gave me a little chewing out, a lot of coaching, a little cheering, and sent me back onto the field. His strategy seemed to be making the competition tougher and tougher until I had to toughen up or die. To the glory of God, I have made most of my plays since then.

Sometimes they're awkward, late, and not very pretty, . . . but the points still count.

Are you still living? Then there's still time on the clock. Are you still a Christian? (And I would remind you that God doesn't abandon His children [Phil. 1:6].) Then you haven't been taken off the team. Get up and fight! God wants to prove to the kingdom of hell that you *will* get up and you *will* prove faithful to God. You must! Those who have been *wholeheartedly, sincerely, and purely devoted to Christ,* no matter how they've been knocked down, will not stay under that pile of opposing players. They *will* call upon the power of their God and get up. And the players of hell will go flying. I really like that part. Maybe because I owe them some massive hits.

Somehow I am helped when I remember that a battle between the Kingdom of God and the kingdom of darkness is going on around me and I might momentarily be called on to make a play. The old spirit of competition kicks in, and it brings the Rudy right out in me. I am utterly amazed at the character of Job to remain so faithful when he had never even seen *Rudy.* Then again, I reckon he wrote the book.

Job provides the primary Old Testament story of God's permissive will for Satan to unleash a full-scale attack on the redeemed. What about the New Testament? Ah, now that one's easy. It happened to one of my best friends.

You have to understand, if I'm writing a Bible study, I don't get out much. Sometimes I spend more time back in the world of Scripture than I do out in my own. I have a feeling God thinks I'm safer if I stay inside. He's proved right. Through the years, some of these Bible figures have become like good buddies. Peter's one of them. He's given me a lot of hope through the years. He spent a lot of his time with Christ big on passion and small on smarts. Been there.

Of course, Peter did have some *huge* moments, like when Christ asked His disciples, "But what about you? . . . Who do you say that I am?" (Matt. 6:15). Peter moved right up to the front of the class. "You are the Christ, the Son of the living God" (v. 16). Now, get a load of this, and don't you dare ruin it by reading it like you've read it a thousand times! Really take it in.

> Jesus replied, "Blessed are you, Simon son of Jonah, for this was not revealed to you by man, but by my Father in heaven. And I tell you that you are Peter, and on this rock I will build my church, and the gates of Hades will not overcome it. I will give you the keys of the kingdom of heaven; whatever you bind on earth will be bound in heaven, and whatever you loose on earth will be loosed in heaven." (Matt. 16:17–19)

Wow. No matter what our differing doctrinal stands may be, surely that's big by any of our standards. The church is built on Jesus Christ (1 Cor. 3:11) and the testimony the disciples would preach concerning Him (Matt. 28:19), but there is no doubt Christ was going to make Peter a major player.

The next thing you know, Peter's shaking his rebuking finger in the face of Jesus Christ for telling them that He (Christ) had many things to suffer, then He'd be killed. In another startling moment that I hope to see on celestial video, Jesus turned and said to Peter,

"Get behind me, Satan! You are a stumbling block to me; you do not have in mind the things of God, but the things of men."

Fast forward to the time when the things Christ prophesied that very day began their fulfillment. Christ and His disciples had just shared the Passover meal, and He had told them that one among them would betray Him. They began questioning who would ever do such a thing, then the discussion descended into a dispute about *which of them was considered to be greatest.*

> "Simon, Simon, Satan has asked to sift you as wheat. But I have prayed for you, Simon, that your faith may not fail. And when you have turned back, strengthen your brothers."
>
> But he replied, "Lord, I am ready to go with you to prison and to death."
>
> Jesus answered, "I tell you, Peter, before the rooster crows today, you will deny three times that you know me." (Luke 22:31–34)

Within only a few hours . . .

> A servant girl saw him seated there in the firelight. She looked closely at him and said, "This man was with him."
>
> But he denied it. "Woman, I don't know him," he said.
>
> A little later someone else saw him and said, "You also are one of them."

"Man, I am not!" Peter replied.

About an hour later another asserted, "Certainly this fellow was with him, for he is a Galilean."

Peter replied, "Man, I don't know what you're talking about!" Just as he was speaking, the rooster crowed. The Lord turned and looked straight at Peter. Then Peter remembered the word the Lord had spoken to him: "Before the rooster crows today, you will disown me three times." And he went outside and wept bitterly. (Luke 22:56–62)

Perhaps this account is familiar to many of us, but the implications are huge to anyone who considers himself or herself a follower, even a disciple, of Jesus Christ. Again, we see that Satan had to attain permission to move outside his usual perimeters and launch a full-scale attack on one of God's children: "Simon, Simon, Satan has asked to sift you as wheat" (v. 31). To me, the fact that permission was granted is utterly obvious in Christ's use of the word "*when* you have turned back, strengthen your brothers" (emphasis mine).

What basic facts can we compile from Job's long nightmare and this unparalleled moment in Peter's life? How could those facts help us with our present subject matter?

First, we see that Satan can and does seek permission to launch excessive attacks on the children of God. Second, we see that God can and sometimes does grant Satan such permission.

But wait a minute. I thought Christ was always *for us*. If He knew Peter was going to blow the play, why did He let the opposition come at him like that? Both Job and Peter were *wholeheartedly, sincerely, and purely devoted* men of God. Agreed? We've never claimed that those who are *wholeheartedly, sincerely, and purely devoted to Christ* are *perfect*. No mortal is. Certainly Peter didn't have Job's maturity, but he was a sincere follower of Jesus Christ who had left family and occupation behind to follow Christ. You didn't see the rest of the disciples take a few steps on the water, did you? I'd say Peter qualified for *wholehearted, sincere, and pure devotion*.

Peter's devotion was pure even when some of the rest of his character needed a little work. He was a pretty good guy. Of course, I'm partial. He's a good friend of mine.

All bias aside, both men had something important in common: they were each tested *by* God *through* Satan. (Is that a scary thought, or what?) I'd like to suggest that Peter's encounter with the evil one wasn't just a *test*. Scripture promises we *all* will be tested so that we can be refined like gold. If you don't believe me, check it out for yourself in Job 23:10 and 1 Peter 1:7. Do you suppose it was a coincidence that God inspired both Job and Peter to pen the analogy of refining like gold?

Hopefully no other child of God will ever have to endure the totality of Job's testing, but none of us will escape some degree of it. I'm suggesting, however, that Peter's test was of a specific variety: it was a *sift*. Dear child of God, this is critically important. Only one reason exists why God would give Satan permission to sift a dearly loved, devoted disciple of Jesus Christ: because *something needs sifting*.

I don't even want you to read further until you have completely absorbed that statement. I am convinced with everything in me that God's answer to Satan's petition to sift Peter as wheat would have been denied had Peter not contained something that needed sifting.

Way back in Matthew 16, we saw that Peter had an awesome call of Christ on his life. Christ even called him by his new name, *Petros*. A chip off the old block. Before the dust could settle and Peter could tell the *Mrs.* what Christ had said, the same Jesus blurted, "Get behind me, Satan!" *Had* Christ made a mistake in choosing Peter? Was He sorry He had? Hardly. He'd made no mistake. Peter was the first disciple to be called and the first to be named an apostle (Mark 1:16–18, 3:14–16). Christ knew exactly what He was doing. He also knew that Peter would react to the news about His death with a rebuke. Furthermore, He knew Peter and the other disciples would lapse into an embarrassing dispute about who was greatest among them at their final meal together. Christ knew every single thing each disciple could do . . . and was capable of doing.

Here's the awesome part of it: Christ obligated Himself to making His true followers what He called them to be. Actually, He still does. Christ told Peter that he would be a powerhouse in the early church, and He meant it. Christ also knew that Peter had no means whatsoever of becoming the person He had called him to be. Like all of us, Peter was far too weak in his natural self (Rom. 6:19). I want you to look carefully at 1 Thessalonians 5:23–24. These verses will become important to us in part 2, but I want to already pave the way for what we're going to learn by applying them to Peter.

May God Himself, the God of peace, sanctify you through and through. May your whole
spirit, soul and body be kept blameless at the
coming of our Lord Jesus Christ. *The one who
calls you is faithful and he will do it.* (emphasis
mine)

Christ called Peter knowing every flaw in him. He gave that
flawed apostle a new assignment and a new name to go with it
and, by heaven, the call would be accomplished even if Christ
had to do it Himself. I believe Jesus loved Peter's passion, but
His cherished disciple also had some ingredients that could
prove less palatable to the call. I'd like to suggest that everything
standing between Simon the fisherman and Peter the Rock
needed to go.

Satan had a sieve. Christ had a purpose. The two collided.
Satan got used. Peter got sifted. "Simon, Simon, Satan has asked
to sift you as wheat." For reasons only our wise, trustworthy God
knows, the most effective and long-lasting way He could get the
Simon out of Peter was a sifting by Satan. He was right. You see,
the One who called us *is* faithful, and He will do whatever it
takes to sanctify us to fulfill our callings. Yes, it's that important.
Remember, there are huge things going on out there that we just
don't understand.

To me, the sifting of Peter can easily and with sound theology be compared to a full-scale attack by Satan on those
with *wholehearted, sincere, and pure devotion to Christ.* In some
ways, Peter's situation was in a league of its own considering
he was the backbone of the brand-new Hebrew-Christian

church. On the other hand, Christ loves all of us with every-thing in Him. No, we're not among those first disciples, but you and I have been called to be disciples or followers of Christ in our own generations. He is just as watchful and pro-tective over *us*.

I believe God allows Satan a certain amount of leash where believers are concerned, but I am convinced that if he wants more than his daily allowance, he has to get permission. None of us is of less importance to Christ than Peter, John, or the apostle Paul. He would never take lightly one of Satan's attacks on His follow-ers. For Satan to launch a full-scale attack of seduction on a *wholehearted, sincere, and purely devoted* follower of Christ, you bet I believe he has to get permission.

So now we return to the original question in our present chapter: Why in the world would God allow someone with a wholehearted and sincere and pure devotion to Christ to get caught in the snare of demonic seduction? I bet you're ready to answer that question now. Because, not unlike Peter, *some-thing* needs removing, sifting, or changing that an intense encounter with the kingdom of hell would best accomplish. I believe this with all my heart, first of all, because it is congru-ent with Scripture, and second, because I am convinced it happened to me.

In the book *Praying God's Word,* I shared about my sifting sea-son with a little more detail, but I think a condensed version could be helpful right here. By almost anyone's standards, I have had some pretty hard challenges in my life, but nothing has ever equaled the intensity and overwhelming sense of darkness that my sifting season did.

Years ago, the ladies in my weekday Bible study class began needling me about writing a Bible study. At that point, I was only preparing weekly lectures, and I had never even considered such a thing. I turned them down on the spot and told them to get themselves to Bible Study Fellowship or a Precept study. (By the way, I *still* tell people that.) They stayed after me until I finally succumbed to the pure pressure of it.

I went before God, sensed His blessing, and decided to give it a try. As I live and breathe, the thought of ever having anything published never even occurred to me then. I absolutely loved what I was already doing and was simply trying to offer this little slice of the Body of Christ what they were asking. I look back on it now and marvel over my naiveté. I had all the passion of David dancing down the streets of Jerusalem—all the passion but no wall of protection around my temple. A big mouth for Jesus with virtually no armor is like a red flag waving at a demon-possessed bull.

In spite of me, God blessed our journey through the Word together, and Satan became infuriated. I think he was fairly certain he had taken care of me a long time ago. He was pretty sure someone with all my junk would never pose him much of a problem, but, you see, the Word of God unleashes a power even in the weakest of us.

We would all be wiser to realize that Satan hates nothing more than the Word of God because it's the Sword of the Spirit. From the evil one's perspective, only one thing appears worse than someone who equips him- or herself with the Word—someone who convinces others to equip themselves too. Of course, I was too green to realize the threat at the time.

In retrospect, I believe Satan asked for permission to get to me, and God held him off until I finished writing the study. Literally within twenty-four hours of putting a period on the last sentence, the enemy began a scheme to destroy me that stands unparalleled in my life. In a nutshell, for a series of months my mind was bombarded with horrible pictures stemming from my childhood. A flood of memories came back to me. Satan proceeded to seduce me into believing horrible lies about myself and virtually everyone I knew. I became physically ill, suffered recurring nightmares, and sank into my own brand of depression. He played such tricks on me that I became convinced I was losing my mind. It was a horrible time of defeat. Had I not loved my children so much, I would've wanted God just to take me home and save me the pain of living. I bet some of you can relate.

Satan had also come after me when I first surrendered to ministry at eighteen, but he was much madder the second time. The first time around, I didn't even know it was *him*. This time around, I *felt* the darkness. I had been serving God with every ounce of energy I had. I was trying to be a godly wife. I was raising my children to love the Lord. Why would God let such a mean thing happen to me? Oh, beloved, because this little woman had something that needed sifting.

Allow me to draw back to my fellow Bible study writers, Henry Blackaby and T. W. Hunt. All three of us will go through various tests because we each need refining. None of us are finished being refined until we're conformed into the image of Christ. While all three of us need refining, all three of us haven't necessarily needed *sifting*. The apostle John didn't appear to need such severe sifting. Neither did James. But Peter did. *And so did I.*

I bet if we asked the dear pastor I talked about earlier if in retrospect he felt that God had sifted anything out of his life, he'd say yes. If nothing else, the pure misunderstanding of other's temptations.

Without question I know what God was sifting out of this servant: *the victim.* I had been a victim in one way or another, forced or self-imposed, my whole life. That woman needed to die and be put out of her misery. God allowed me to be so totally victimized by the devil's schemes and my own well-hidden lack of emotional health that I would allow God to do *whatever necessary* to make me whole.

My recovery took a while. I don't mind telling you it was one painful journey, but I wouldn't trade what He accomplished for anything on earth. I absolutely could not have gone to the places of ministry God had planned in the shape I was in, no matter how well I dressed it.

The peculiar thing was, I had no idea how unhealthy I was. I had kept it covered underneath a cloak of activity, but nothing in all creation is hidden from God's sight. In His severe and loving mercy, in ways I'll never fully understand, God used the darkness to chase out my darkness, then filled the emptied vessel with light. No matter how many years it's been, I still have the conscious thought almost every day, *So, this is how it feels to be free.* What Satan meant for evil, my faithful God meant for good.

Beloved, are you being sifted? Has God permitted the enemy to launch a full-scale attack against you? God knows what He's doing. He isn't looking the other way, and He's not being mean to you. Maybe this is the only way He can get you to attend to the old so He can do something new. Grab onto Him for dear life! Give Him full reign to remove anything in you that needs to go. Hasten the end of the process. Sift, dear one. *Sift!*

PART II

THE
WATCHMAN

CHAPTER 6

SEDUCE-PROOFING OUR LIVES

We have one primary purpose throughout part 2: To learn to the best of our biblical knowledge how to seduce-proof our lives. This portion of the book applies to any believer regardless of spiritual maturity. It also applies no matter how *wholehearted, sincere, and pure* your devotion to Christ may be. In fact, you may discover through these pages why certain riches and fulfillments of the Christian faith have somehow eluded you. Keep in mind that the chief goal of all seduction is to woo us to the false loves of lesser gods so that they may then gleefully betray us.

We won't have to go an inch further than this chapter to discover the secret to seduce-proofing our lives. All subsequent chapters will teach us specific ways to do what a single passage of Scripture suggests. I don't think for a moment that what I'm offering on these pages is conclusive. My hope is that authors and men and women of God who are far wiser than I will do further research and teach seeking laity like me. Oh, that others who know much would tell us all the more!

Our focal Scripture throughout part 1 has been 2 Corinthians 11:2–3. I hope you've practically memorized it by now. In the previous chapter, I hinted what our focal passage will be throughout part 2. First Thessalonians 5:23–24 holds the key that locks the gate where seduction creeps in. Read these two verses with great care; then I wonder if you would consider memorizing them over the next several days. If we'll allow God to write this segment of Scripture in permanent marker on our hearts, even if our ships get off course and we find ourselves in an ocean of vulnerability, it will serve as a lighthouse to guide us back to safe harbor.

> May God himself, the God of peace, sanctify
> you through and through. May your whole spirit,
> soul and body be kept blameless at the coming of
> our Lord Jesus Christ. The one who calls you is
> faithful and he will do it. (1 Thess. 5:23–24)

In these verses, the terms *spirit, soul,* and *body* are meant to encompass every part of our lives. In fact, I am convinced that the very essence of wholeness is when our whole spirit, soul, and body are sanctified through and through. You may ask, "Where is the reference to the heart and the mind?" In this verse, both are implied in the concept of the soul. Our spirits give us the capacity to know, hear, and have a relationship with God. When differentiated from the spirit, the soul encompasses everything else immaterial about us.

By faith start thinking of these two verses as the heart of everything we need for protection from seduction. Take time to copy them on a card so you can memorize them. Toward the end of this chapter, we'll discover why they are so critical. Until then, I want you to look at this same "heart" with its surrounding tissues and ligaments.

We're going to widen our scope on this powerful chapter by looking at 1 Thessalonians 5:16–25. In these verses we find one of the most concentrated segments of Scripture in the entire New Testament that describes exactly what you and I are looking for: a seduce-proofed believer. To get the full effect, we'll stick this well-protected believer in the extra large context of the Amplified Bible. Inspect this description carefully because you and I want to look like this sooner than later.

> Be happy [in your faith] and rejoice and be glad-hearted continually—always. Be unceasing in prayer—praying perseveringly;
> Thank [God] in everything—no matter what the circumstances may be, be thankful and give thanks; for this is the will of God for you [who are] in Christ Jesus [the Revealer and Mediator of that will].
> Do not quench (suppress or subdue) the (Holy) Spirit;
> Do not spurn the gifts and utterances of the prophets—do not depreciate prophetic revelations nor despise inspired instruction or exhortation or warning.
> But test and prove all things [until you can recognize] what is good; [to that] hold fast.

Abstain from evil—shrink from it and keep
aloof from it—in whatever form or whatever kind
it may be.

And may the God of peace Himself sanctify
you through and through—separate you from pro-
fane things, make you pure and wholly consecrated to God—and may your spirit and soul and
body be preserved sound and complete [and
found] blameless at the coming of our Lord Jesus
Christ, the Messiah.

Faithful is He Who is calling you [to Himself]
and utterly trustworthy, and He will also do it
[fulfill His call by hallowing and keeping you].

Brethren, pray for us.

A Concise Profile of a Seduce-Proofed Christian

This powerful passage of Scripture provides us a picture of
what a seduce-proofed life looks like. Let's consider each element
of this description. First note of the seduce-proofed believer:

1. He is happy in his faith.

I want to shout hallelujah with you before I even have a
chance to explain what we have to shout about! Dear one, when
was the last time someone fairly balanced in Scripture told you
that this faith thing isn't only about sacrifices and continually
delayed gratification? The apostle Paul seemed to be saying, "For

heaven's sake, be happy in your faith! That's one reason you have it!" Let's take this opportunity to expose another good example of a doctrine of demons. Too many of us have somehow come to believe that we lack maturity if we wish that the Christian life wasn't just good for us like a bowl of bran but that it could also occasionally make us happy like a chocolate malt!

That voice in your ear has been lying all this time. Guess what? You have complete biblical permission to be happy in your faith and also to do the unthinkable—be bold enough to ask *why* if you're not!

Some of our dear brothers and sisters around the world are so terribly persecuted for their Christian beliefs that they may have a greater challenge being happy in their faith. Many of them live and die as martyrs and *then* enter their "master's happiness." If you have the freedom to read a Christian book like this one, however, then you are living in enough freedom where being *happy in your faith* can be a reality more often than not. In fact, a primary reason we are vulnerable to seduction after we have received the Spirit of Christ is that we misunderstand what we've been given. We continue to look for happiness outside of Christ.

We're going to discover that the characteristic of happiness in the seduce-proofed Christian is tied to another element in the list. Therefore, I'm going to pull it out of scriptural order and give it to you next.

2. She abstains from evil.

You see, the greatest source of God-given power you and I will have to *abstain from evil* is to *be happy in our faith*. Certainly many other things can add happiness to our lives, but they are detoxified and made safe to the believer when her primary source of happiness is faith in Jesus. Without happiness in Christ, any other source of joy can become a tool for seduction.

I grew up thinking Christianity and going to church were all about what we "didn't do." The serpent came and beguiled me just as he did Eve and deceived me into thinking that at least I could feel alive if I did what I wasn't supposed to do. I think back on some of my young years and wonder how I made it without someone snatching me bald-headed. My family lived across from the high school when I was in elementary school. My older sister and I were such a handful that when we wanted to play school, we broke in to the high school to do it. Just the fact that it was locked made Gay and me want to break in.

Think about this with me: only one tree in the entire Garden was forbidden to Adam and Eve. Instead of surveying everything God had given her and marveling, *All of this!* the serpent seduced Eve into thinking, *Perhaps I'd rather trade in all of this for the one thing that God has told me to avoid. He could be holding out on me.*

Believer, the serpent has sold us such a lie, and we have paid dearly for it. In comparison to all we've been given to enjoy in our earthly life with Christ, what we've been called to avoid is like one measly tree in the whole garden. The trouble is, we don't even begin to eat of the fruit in the endless groves of our garden. Ephesians 1:3 says we have *every spiritual blessing* in Christ!

We reach for the fruit of forbidden trees because we're getting a little bored with a steady diet of nothing but apples and bananas. Some of us haven't widened our spiritual horizons in decades. We are doing exactly the same things to fuel our

Christian faith that we did years ago, and we're in a rut. A spiritual rut is fertile ground for seduction. It's time we wake up and smell the guava! We haven't made it to the mangoes and papayas yet. When you and I start taking Christ up on all He made possible for us, we will be so much happier *in our faith* that *abstaining from evil* will not seem nearly so sacrificial.

Abstaining from evil used to be hard for me in my adolescent years, and no wonder it was! An unsatisfied soul, an empty abyss, is nothing but a stronghold waiting to happen. When we learn to really enjoy our God and His endless benefits, the unhealthy need we had for carnal pleasures is diffused. The need has already been met just as it was meant to be. Nothing will make you happier on a more consistent basis than a full-bore, flood-stage relationship with Jesus Christ.

I have a dear friend who was raised in an extremely strict home. Her father was a pastor and forbade his family to celebrate any of the silliness of Christmas or Easter, and they were never allowed to see a movie or a theatrical performance. And goodness knows a fiery destiny would have awaited them had they dared attend the high school homecoming dance. He took everything pleasurable away from them in the name of abstaining from evil, but he gave them absolutely nothing in its place. I can almost see Christ leaning over the edge of heaven yelling, "What in the world are you doing?"

To them Jesus became the God of the Big No.

Again the apostle Paul wrote:

> But as surely as God is faithful, our message to
> you is not "Yes" and "No." For the Son of God,

Jesus Christ, who was preached among you by me and Silas and Timothy, was not "Yes" and "No," but in him it has always been "Yes." For no matter how many promises God has made, they are "Yes" in Christ. And so through him the "Amen" is spoken by us to the glory of God. (2 Cor. 1:18–20)

The reason we are so pulled to the No's is because we have never filled our lives to the flood stage with the Yes! Sure, there are No's. *Abstain from evil.* But we won't be nearly as tempted when we're happy in our faith, rejoicing and glad-hearted. We have a "Yes" God who says no only to things that aren't worthy of His children and don't fit into their own personal "1 Corinthians 2:9s." (I'm not going to give it away. You'll have to look it up. And when you do, write your name by it. That's exactly what God wants your reality to be.) After your side trip, notice what else is characteristic of the protected Christian:

3. He is unceasing in prayer.

Don't freak out on me here. Once we grasp some of the meaning of this phrase, we'll see that the pursuit of it is not out of our reach. We've been so indoctrinated by certain definitions of prayer that all the words "praying unceasingly" mean to us is that the preacher lost his mind and called on Brother Hubert to give the benediction at the end of the service. Halfway through the endless droning, even God wanted to go to the cafeteria.

By "praying unceasingly" Paul really didn't have in mind our repetitive, wearying formulas. He was talking about a perpetual line of open communication with God throughout the entire day. We're not given to this kind of mentality naturally, so I'm convinced that we have to learn *how* to pray unceasingly. Mind you, this one will be an ongoing pursuit and one we aren't likely to master, but isn't prayer just that? *A pursuit?*

I have picked up on the terminology of Brother Lawrence, who called praying unceasingly *practicing God's presence.* In fact, practicing God's presence has been my number one goal for the last year. It simply means to develop a constant awareness of God's presence all the time. When we live with such awareness, we as naturally pick up a conversation with God at any given moment in a day as we would with someone sitting a few feet from us.

Maybe this example will help: A friend lost her husband of many years to death. She says she still catches herself talking to him. The difference is, when we talk to God He is *always* there. It's called omnipresence.

A pray-without-ceasing relationship means seeing everything against the backdrop of His presence. In other words, a rain shower reminds us of Him. A difficulty at work makes us turn our thoughts to Him. The first bite of pecan pie makes us thank the God who gave us the gift of taste. A near-empty gas tank keeps us hanging tight with God as we coast on fumes to the station. Everything and anything. Even listening to a powerful worship CD while you're putting dishes in the dishwasher is prayer without ceasing. Constant communication. Sometimes saying a lot, sometimes saying a little, but living every moment of life as if He is right there. After all, isn't He?

So what does unceasing communication have to do with protecting ourselves from the enemy? Ah, how often do loneliness and insecurity open a soul for seduction? Our next exhortation, however, actually helps greatly to combat loneliness and insecurity.

4. She is thankful and gives thanks.

Seduce-proofed people live lives of active gratitude. When we've turned the last page of this book, one fact I pray that every one of us will know by heart is that dissatisfaction is a stronghold waiting to happen. An unsatisfied soul should never be ignored. Ongoing or chronic feelings of dissatisfaction are waving red flags that need to be well inspected. Such feelings may mean something vital is missing, and we need to seek God without delay.

Other times, nagging feelings of dissatisfaction can be little more than the by-product of living in such an overindulged society. Think about it. Countless millions of dollars are spent annually by advertisers whose only goal is to convince Americans that we are not yet satisfied. Since our hearts are deceptive in their natural form, sometimes our feelings are telling us we're less satisfied than we really are.

How can we know the difference? Apply the phrase Paul supplied us: "Be thankful and give thanks." Active gratitude will cure self- or society-induced dissatisfaction. Often we know what our problem *is*. We even know what the *remedy* may be. If we're going to learn to seduce-proof our lives, we're going to have to start taking the medicine the Word prescribes when we're spiritually feeling under the weather.

Many times we don't have a knowledge problem; we have an obedience problem. *Be thankful and give thanks.* Do you hear what Paul is saying? Just trying to sit like a thankful-looking bump on a dead log won't cut it. *Actively give thanks.*

When I'm feeling down or a little like a brat, I often sense God speaking to my heart, "Name 'em, child." I don't even have to ask what He means. He means start naming a mere twenty or thirty of the thousands of ways He's shown His goodness to me. God has had such mercy on my life, I ought to be among the most grateful people on the earth, and that's exactly what I want to be.

God has taught me another way to actively give thanks. He has shown His goodness to me in innumerable ways through other people. I sense Him saying to me, "Give thanks to Me first and foremost, but, Beth, I want you to be one of the most genuine and vocally grateful people others know. I have caused many people to show you kindness and help you accomplish your calling. Thank them continually." I am sure the same is true of your life. God is teaching me not just to be thankful for the love and support I receive from my family, my staff, my friends, and my church but to actively *tell* them.

If our selfish hearts are trying to trick us into feeling a false sense of dissatisfaction, a good strong dose of thanksgiving will cure what ails us! If it doesn't, we've got a more serious issue, and we must diligently seek the wisdom and remedy of God.

5. He doesn't quench the Spirit.

Nothing will be more important to us in seduce-proofing our lives than practicing the Holy Spirit–filled or *controlled* life. We're going to discover that we are absolutely incapable of consistent victory on our own. *Half-filled* is still *half-empty.* Without the full empowerment of the Holy Spirit, we have no defense whatsoever against the enemy's schemes.

We're up against demonic powers and principalities! The wicked biggies! If you'll allow me to default to comfortable terminology, this ain't small potatoes we're dealing with here. The only spirit that can overcome seducing spirits is the Holy Spirit. When we quench Him, we're standing in front of Goliath with God whispering into our hard little heads, "I think you might need to know that you're basically on your own here. If you need any help, let Me know."

I can't resist sharing the NIV translation for this exhortation: "Do not put out the Spirit's fire." May I say that if our churches are boring, it's not the Holy Spirit's fault? He brings along plenty of fire if we'll refrain from training our leaders to be volunteer firemen. In all fairness, many a leader has a fire-lit soul, but some of the rest of them sure are handy with a water hose.

Whether we realize it or not, God formed every one of us with a wick just waiting to be lit. He created us for the fire of the Holy Spirit! If we quench His fire, we'll look for another one elsewhere. That's when we're liable to get burned. I'm certainly not implying sensual passions alone. Anger, rage, and all manner of lusts are also counterfeit passions or self-built fire starters.

Think back for a moment to a scene captured in Exodus chapter 3. I love that Moses heard the voice of God coming from a burning bush. The fire itself was not what made Moses want to take a second look. A fire wasn't unusual. Lightning could easily have sparked a flame. Exodus 3:3 specifies why Moses moved in a little closer: "So Moses thought, 'I will go over and see this strange sight—why the bush does not burn up.'"

Good point

What made the fire unusual was that the flames were not burning up the bush. Hebrews 12:29 says that our God is "a consuming fire." You see, God's is the only fire that can consume an object without eventually destroying it. *Anger destroys. Rage destroys. Lust destroys.* God's fire isn't destructive. He doesn't feed off of us. He is the I Am, the self-existent One. He invites us to feed off of Him. No other fiery passion in our souls will ever guard us from getting burned. Now notice the next exhortation:

6. She does not despise instruction, exhortation, or warning.

This point is *huge*. Not only is the seduce-proofed individual a hearer and doer of the Word, he is also a man (or woman, of course) who does not despise the instructions, exhortations, or warnings of those whom God sends his way.

I hate regrets, don't you? I hate looking back at some mistakes I have made and remembering warnings I chose to ignore. I'm not alone. Remember that one of the common claims of the seduced was failing to heed an early warning.

Keep in mind that these instructions, exhortations, or warnings may not come face-to-face. They may come from a sermon, a Christian radio broadcast, or a Christian book that God has purposely placed in our hands. They may also come from a source less agreeable to our palates.

Don't go acting as if you have no idea what I mean. Don't you just hate when someone you don't even particularly like is *right*? Not only do I like to pick out the advice I want; I like to pick out who gives it to me! God doesn't always send our favorite messengers with His well-pointed exhortations. We have to learn to listen anyway. We need to be desperate for good advisers, and we also need to be desperate for the humility to receive instruction.

Sometimes we may receive a warning or an exhortation from a godly source that leads us to forego what seemed like a wonderful opportunity. Later we may find ourselves troubled by resentful feelings, wondering if we should have gone against the counsel. Of course, we are always wise to pray diligently through these kinds of conflicts to make absolutely sure any human counsel lines up with God's counsel. If we believe it does—even when we don't want it to—we must *rest in it* and try to avoid second-guessing it. We may have no idea until heaven the calamity we avoided.

If the counsel of the wise seems to match the sense you're getting from the Holy Spirit after much prayer, go with their advice no matter how badly your flesh wants to do otherwise!

7. He tests and proves all things until he recognizes what is good.

This characteristic is the perfect follow-up to our previous one. If we'll learn to test and prove all things, we'll also come to agreement with God-sent exhortation or warning. I can't think of many characteristics more vital in the profile of the seduce-proofed man or woman.

If we're going to start practicing well-fortified lives, we might need to recognize that the muscle this point represents tends to be weak in most of us. We need to ask God to strengthen it. Keep in mind that He'll probably fortify it the most natural way muscles are strengthened: *through exercise and repetition.*

Developing this characteristic has been a challenge for me. My embarrassingly impulsive and impatient nature aggravated my former poor discernment. To my natural personality, practically anything "positive" sounded like a great idea to me! Can anyone relate?

Now I know that good and evil do not always appear black-and-white in our technicolor world. Furthermore, a huge chasm can separate goodwill from God's will. I'm slowly learning to test and prove all things *until* I can recognize what is good. I still find the wait excruciating at times.

Poor discernment, impulsiveness, and impatience can be a disastrous threesome, and I have paid for their group effort more than a few times. I am actively trying to fire them. They have not served me well. As we learn to take ownership over our weaknesses, I hope we're all going to fire a few things that haven't served us well.

Before we go to the last few characteristics in our profile of a seduce-proofed life, does anyone need a breather? Perhaps right about now someone is thinking, *Good grief! Don't we get any life to ourselves? Do we just have to be eaten up with Jesus?* Nope. We don't have to be eaten up with Jesus. We can be eaten up by the roaring lion instead. Based on what I'm witnessing, we can basically take our pick. One or the other is most likely going to happen.

You see, where we're headed on the Kingdom calendar we will be increasingly surrounded by deception (which will always mean increasing strongholds) and wickedness (which will always mean increasing temptations). Double-minded Christians aren't going to lose their eternal inheritance, but they are going to be eaten alive on this earth.

I'll just go ahead and say it. I *am* suggesting that we be "eaten up" with Jesus, but if that seems too radical for you, I hope you'll give me a chance to show you what it means through the remainder of part 2. Actually, God's way can be the biggest blast of your life. You may be in for a shock. You may discover that you don't have to be miserable and pent-up to be safe.

I am so sad that many equate deep spirituality only with going to church or sitting motionless in our prayer closets. I love church, and I certainly couldn't live without prayer. I believe in practicing the vital, life-giving disciplines of Bible study, prayer, meditation, worship, and fasting. But in addition to the good, strong backbone they provide, I also believe in a lot of ribs reaching out from them.

I think God is perfectly comfortable at a kid's soccer game. I think He gets a huge kick out of the sidesplitting belly laughs of His children. I think He nods approvingly over a good, uncompromising novel and sings quietly over us when we take a nice, long Sunday afternoon nap. He is the God of *life*. Every single part of it. When we compartmentalize God, we may be noble and religious enough to put Him in the very top drawer, but all the other drawers are open targets without Him.

Throughout our present chapter, we've been drawing a profile of a seduce-proofed believer. Now we've arrived at the very issue that sets this Christian apart and protects him or her from innumerable schemes. All of the other characteristics in the profile are manifestations that this believer does one vital thing:

8. She allows God Himself to sanctify her through and through.

There you have it. *Through and through.* By the time we get to the end of this book, I hope those three words turn over in your mind like a broken record. Our safety, our joy, our fulfillment, and our wholeness are all found in allowing God to completely invade our "through and through." Nothing withheld. Nothing off-limits. No part of our lives from birth to death. No part of our beings from conscious to subconscious. No part of our minds. No part of our emotions. *Through and through.*

Why have I fallen for some of Satan's schemes in the past? Because something in my "through and through" wasn't utterly sanctified to God. I don't mean perfected. I just mean surrendered and under the safekeeping of His dominion. Sanctification basically means set apart. Anything of our experiences, issues, or weaknesses that we don't deliberately *set apart* to the safekeeping of Christ's dominion sits like a wide-open target under the nose of the lion.

As I shared a bit of my testimony, I told you that Satan was able to attack me because I had not surrendered my past to God. Yes, I really do believe to the best of my understanding that I was *wholeheartedly, sincerely, and purely devoted to Christ*— but I wasn't sanctified *through and through.* I kept the basement locked. Get the picture? If not, that's OK. The following chapters will make it much clearer. Each one will give you a few more crayons to fill in the picture of Jesus joyfully and protectively filling the life of a flesh-and-blood mortal *through and through.*

Before we can go on, however, we have a couple more elements to look at from 1 Thessalonians 5. Next, note the ninth characteristic I desire for my life:

9. His whole spirit, soul, and body are kept blameless.

I sure like the sound of that! Throughout part 2 we will be discussing how to guard ourselves against seduction, but I want you to hear something before we go a step further. If we have to be perfect (and by that I mean *sinless*) to be protected, we may as well throw in the towel. If that were true, we may just as well all chant, "Even so, Lord Jesus, come quickly!"

Perfection in this lifetime is *not* going to happen. Anyway, believe it or not, I don't think Christ's perfection was the primary guard He had against seduction. His primary guard was that He was totally fulfilled by His Father's love, presence, and will. Developing perfection is not a reasonable or expected earthly hope for mortals, but I'll tell you what *can* be the goal: *Blamelessness!*

Paul wrote, "May your whole spirit, soul and body be kept blameless" (1 Thess. 5:23).

Recently I taught portions of the Book of Psalms in my Sunday school class. The psalmists speak often of this coveted condition they describe as "blameless." Proverbs 28:18 tells us something about being blameless that makes it terribly pertinent to our present subject matter: "He whose walk is blameless is kept safe."

Bingo! That's exactly what we are looking for. How can we be *kept safe* from seduction? By developing a blameless walk. Now don't put the book down. I know you tire of hearing one impossible dream after another from churchy people, but this one really is attainable. God revealed a Scripture to me that defines a very livable *blamelessness*. We've already seen its context in a previous chapter.

> Who can discern his errors?
>   Forgive my hidden faults.
> Keep your servant also from willful sins;   *Jesus*
>   may they not rule over me.
> Then will I be blameless,
>   innocent of great transgression. (Ps. 19:12–13)

What is David's inspired definition of blamelessness? When no willful sin is *ruling* over us. Living out from under the dominion of willful sin is not only possible; it is our God-given right, our Holy Spirit–empowered reality, and the absolute will of our Father in heaven.

I *know* this kind of blamelessness is possible because if I can live an extended period of time with it, *anybody can!* It's still a challenge because I tend to want to default to fear and worry in my flesh nature, but blamelessness is not so unreachable that it is frustratingly out of grasp.

Yes, indeed. *He whose walk is blameless is kept safe.* So how do we start becoming blameless? By allowing God Himself to sanctify us through and through! Our relationships, our forms of entertainment, our hobbies, and everything else! Our safety is inviting Christ's involvement in everything. And He's no bore either. He can get a big kick out of watching you play tennis. He wants no sign on any part of our lives to say, *Keep out!* If He's there, Satan can't touch it.

Let's take a look at the remaining two characteristics in our profile of the seduce-proofed man or woman.

10. She knows that the One who called her is faithful and He will do it.

The seduce-proofed woman has no confidence in her flesh. Nor does she dream that checking off a list of characteristics or performing a catalog of spiritual disciplines have any power to protect her. She knows that God is faithful, and *He will do it.*

The seduce-proofed believer simply realizes that obedience places him in the posture God delights to bless. Obedience invites Christ to show His incomparable strength in our mortal weakness.

God wants to and is eager to BLESS

11. He knows he needs prayer.

First Thessalonians 5:25 has only four words in each of the primary Bible translations, but they are powerful!

"Brethren, pray for us."

Egads! I started to overlook this one! What a mistake that would have been! Brothers and sisters, we need prayer. That's all there is to it. Especially as the *Day* is drawing near!

How many people actively intercede for you on a consistent basis? If you can't name at least several, get busy enlisting some! Commit to reciprocate, and become an effective intercessor for others. We need one another's prayers desperately. Don't assume that since you've done OK so far without prayer partners that you're not at risk. These are ever increasing days of wickedness! Start looking.

Commanding us to pray for one another is one of the ways God enforces unity in the Body of Christ. Let's make the most of our intercessors. Tell them specific requests. Humble yourself before them and ask them to pray for the strengthening of weak spiritual muscles. Consider equipping them with Scriptures that you want them to pray will become realities in your life. Unequaled power can be released when we pray Scripture for one another.

As we conclude this chapter, could we practice what Paul just preached to us by example? I want you to know that I am praying for every person God will cause to read this book. He knows your name, your motivation for reading, and the work He wants to accomplish in *you,* even if you're reading to help someone else.

May I ask you to do two things that I am confident God is placing on my heart and will bless? First, please stop right now and pray for someone out there who once had *wholehearted, sincere, and pure devotion to Christ* but is presently caught in a web of seduction. He or she is in such urgent need. Along with any other intercession the Holy Spirit gives you, please pray the following Scriptures for this sister or brother:

> I pray also that the eyes of your heart may be enlightened in order that you may know the hope to which he has called you, the riches of his glorious inheritance in the saints, and his incomparably great power for us who believe. (Eph. 1:18–19)

Pray, according to Ephesians 5:8–15, that this "sleeper" would "wake up" and that God would mercifully expose the deeds of darkness to him or to her and expose the precious life to the light so healing can begin.

Finally, would you pray one time for me? I cannot keep from crying as I ask you to do such a personal thing. Beloved, I cannot even imagine God calling me to do some of the things He has. I will never understand His ways. I have been such a broken vessel and have known such strongholds in my life. That He dares to use me is startling to me. Please pray that I will continue to throw myself before His throne, forsaking all other gods and the approval of men, that my life will be *seduce-proofed,* that I will not lead people in error, and that I would love His Son more than anything in all of life.

Thank you, dear one.

CHAPTER 7

THE SAFE HOUSE
OF LOVE

I got a bit of a late start writing today. Toward the end of the praise and worship service I attended in the den of my cabin this morning (by myself), I heard the voice of God speak to my heart: "Come and play." I love that He said, "Come." Not, "Go." "Come." That meant He was already there.

I also love how I could tell by the sweet tone of the silent voice whispering to my spirit that He was smiling. You know, you can tell that kind of thing in the voices of those you really know. I can tell you the exact expression on my husband or children's faces when I talk to them on the phone just by the pitch of their voices. It was that way this morning. I could have outlined His expression with my finger.

I don't always hear Him like that. Oh, I wish I did, but I don't. Sometimes we have to walk away from the deafening demands of our chaotic lives to inhale His.

I've been writing from early in the morning until late at night. I've been awed by the April snow dancing from the sky as

I watched from the picture window and wrote. I fear I've been too under the weather with what my mother called the "croup" to go out and soak myself in it. Not today. "Come and play." So I did.

I built a snowman. I used grapes for his eyes, and a half-moon-shaped sesame snack made the perfect smile. I didn't give him a nose. I have enough for both of us. He's wearing my hat and scarf, and I rather hope he doesn't get them wet. I let him borrow them because I was coming back inside. I laughed with God. He laughed with me. And now for reasons only the Maker of my silly soul can explain, I cry.

I am so in love with Him. *I am so in love with Him.* We look with pained desperation for things that are already there. The snow was already there. I had just not yet taken it personally. Dear seeker, the breeze is already there. The sunset is already there. The morning tide is already there. The timid doe is already there. The summer rain is already there. Have you taken them personally?

I lived so much of my life having no idea how a mortal heart with eyes blinded to the object of their greatest pleasure could be so slain by immortal romance. I will not rest. Hear me. I will not rest until I have told everyone who will listen of this wondrous love. I am jealous with a godly jealousy for every son and daughter of the living God to know and experience a pulsing, breathing love that exceeds every earthly shadow of the True.

This morning during praise and worship, I climbed the ladder of the tiny loft, opened the window, and sang these words to my God while catching snowflakes in my hand:

My Jesus, my Savior
Lord there is none like You
All of my days I want to praise
The wonders of Your mighty love
My comfort, my shelter
Tower of refuge and strength
Let every breath
All that I am
Never cease to worship You
Shout to the Lord
All the earth let us sing
Power and majesty
Praise to the King
Mountains bow down
And the seas will roar
At the sound of Your Name
I sing for joy at the work of Your hands
Forever I'll love You
Forever I'll stand
Nothing compares
To the promise I have in You.[1]

Do you know the song? Far more important, do you know the love? Have you truly—and do not answer me quickly—discovered that nothing compares? Nothing? Can He do to your heart what no one else can do? Can you feel things with God that you feel with no one else? Have you been slain by His perfect love? Has He ruined you for anyone else? Has He cut the strings on your heart like an air balloon, ascending you above your fear of loving with no return? Has He enabled you to love others more freely and vulnerably than ever before—yet those loves can no longer compare?

Oh, please listen. I could go to the furthest reaches of human vocabulary and study the languages of every people to find who says it best, and still all my efforts would be frustrated by this divine affection that exceeds description. Yet this love, this ravenous love of God, is meant for every mortal creature whose calloused feet have traveled miles of earth to find a carnal affection that suffices.

God waits, watches, and hopes that the sun will not set on our length of days without our standing on tiptoes at the extremity of life, yelling, "Is there not more than this?"

"Ah, yes, my love. There is more."

Oh, beloved, we sing of this love week after week in our perfectly timed orders of worship while heaven's hosts gather curiously and watch masses of mortals sing in one accord of a love they do not know. Angel faces look upon God, then again upon His children. And their eyes, having no human cataract, behold the actual substance of divine love

> as wet as water,
> but not water,
> as weighty and warm as a woolen cloak,
> yet not woolen,
> and as light and distinct as a snowflake,
> but never cold,
> lavished in heaps upon the very mortals who do
> not feel it.

A fury rises within me and my soul shakes its fist. Surely the vilest of all doctrines of demons tells us that love for God—since He is by essence unseen and untouched—is not something you feel. Lies!

What would you tell a new mother with an infant whose cord was cut from her own body just weeks ago who confides in you, "I'm so glad I have her. I waited so long. She is so perfect. So beautiful. I am so grateful she is mine. Truly she has delivered me from my feelings of uselessness and my lack of identity. But I thought I would feel something. I was told I'd feel love. Is it OK that I don't? Is this normal?"

How would you respond? Would you tell her: "Of course your feelings are normal, dear mother! Just rock your baby in your arms and say over and over again, 'I love you.' Sing her love songs. If you say it long enough and loud enough, it will be true. Sing it and maybe you will feel something. It will be love for the song more than love for your baby, but at least you will feel something."

Or would you tell this mother: "Yes, you're perfectly normal. Love for your baby just is. It doesn't really feel. It just is. You can feel love for your neighbor and love for your garden, but love for your baby isn't something you feel. Those who say it is simply conjure it up in their foolish imaginings."

No, indeed! We would tell her to get to her doctor! That something isn't normal. That she might be suffering from post-partum depression. Our hearts would break as we see the tears of lack flowing down her face and we realize that her heart is free to feel guilt but strangely shackled from love. We would hold her in our arms while she weeps. We would also weep as we pray pleadings of God over her, then we would assure her of what we know:

"Dear, dear mother, your heart was made for love. You just do not yet feel it. Do not despair. It is there. You were not made a mother and not given the love. You are so right to have told me. Now all we must do is discover why you do not feel what is yours to feel."

Then we would help her search for the door of her prison. Several years later, we would walk by the park and rejoice to hear the laughter of children. We would stop and watch. Our eyes would fall on a young mother pushing a tiny mass of curls and ribbons on the park swing. We'd grin as the child—delightfully drunk from motion—cackles so unashamedly that her mother bends over, aching with laughter. We'd sense a vague familiarity, then as the moment of knowing finally comes, the tears would sting in our eyes as we realize we are standing, beholding love found.

"You foolish Galatians! Who has bewitched you?" (Gal. 3:1). Who has made us think that all lesser loves, mere shadows of the True, feel while the greater love for which the heart was thus created is not felt? It simply exists. We sing of it. We speak of it. But we do not feel it.

At the risk of offending thousands of people, I will say again what the Spirit of God bellows in my soul: the Bride of Christ suffers from lack of love for her Groom. She admires Him. She respects Him. She is grateful to Him. She's been saved by Him. She is intellectually stimulated by Him. She loves her new clothes. She is enamored by the jewels. But she expected to feel love. Is it OK that she doesn't? Is this normal?

"Of course it is! Go right on singing. Tell everyone you know. They will wonder that something undefined seems to be missing, but if you say it long enough, you will make it true."

The Bride is suffering from post-deliverance depression. She expected to feel something. Is it OK that she doesn't?

> One of the teachers of the law came and heard them debating. Noticing that Jesus had given them a good answer, he asked him, "Of all the commandments, which is the most important?"
>
> "The most important one," answered Jesus, "is this: 'Hear, O Israel, the Lord our God, the Lord is one. Love the Lord your God with all your heart and with all your soul and with all your mind and with all your strength.'"
>
> "Well said, teacher. . . ." (Mark 12:28–32)

Indeed, well said. But you and I are yearning for the words, "Well done." Masses of believers do not realize that love for God is something they can actually feel. In fact, if we don't, we are frighteningly, staggeringly vulnerable to a counterfeit.

I am not suggesting that we feel the constant gush of love for God every waking moment any more than I feel the constant gush of love for my husband and children. Yet, my affection for them is a greater reality than my flesh and bone. There are times, however, when I nearly drown in the gush of divine love and marvel that something so full and so perfect could ever come from something so injured as I.

We experience the first miracle at the wedding of Cana once again every time an earthen pitcher full of water pours forth sweet wine. But will we risk letting the wine evaporate in our generation?

As Jesus was sitting on the Mount of Olives, the disciples came to Him privately. "Tell us," they said, "when will this happen, and what will be the sign of your coming and of the end of the age?"

Jesus answered:

> Watch out that no one deceives you. For many will come in my name, claiming, "I am the Christ," and will deceive many. You will hear of wars and rumors of wars, but see to it that you are not alarmed. Such things must happen, but the end is still to come. Nation will rise against nation, and kingdom against kingdom. There will be famines and earthquakes in various places. All these are the beginning of birth pains. . . . *Because of the increase of wickedness, the love of most will grow cold,* but he who stands firm to the end will be saved. And this gospel of the kingdom will be preached in the whole world as a testimony to all nations, and then the end will come." (Matt. 24:4–8, 12–14, emphasis mine)

One of the most insidious diseases of the latter days will be cold souls. In the above Scripture the word *cold* is our translation of the Greek word *psycho*. "It is from this verb that *psyche,* soul, is derived. Hence psyche is the breath of a living creature, animal life. *Psycho* occurs only once, in the future passive, meaning to be cool, to grow cool or cold in a spiritual sense, as regards Christian love" (Matt. 24:12).[2]

Bride of Christ, we must never tolerate a lack of love in our souls nor let anyone convince us that it is normal not to feel love for God. The Bride was created to love the Groom. Not only is a lack of love for God our heart's most needless tragedy, loving God is our only recourse for divinely loving for others.

I am sick to death of hearing the echo of the teachers of the law, "Well said, teacher!" but never well done. The teacher of the law is scared out of his wits to love for fear something might show beneath his prayer shawl. And, while I'm at it, if I hear another person say, "But we must be careful that we don't start thinking this whole Christian thing is only about feelings," I think I may go crazy.

No, no, no! This whole Christian thing is certainly not only about feelings. I didn't say *feelings*. I said *feeling*. Shall we equate a congregation ravished by love with frenzies and fallouts, shrill laughter and animal sounds? Please! I'm not talking about a hypnotic spiritual high. "Test the spirit!" the apostle John would scold us.

I'm talking about a cavernous soul, a hidden abyss that learns how to open its sullen self to God and knows the crystal-clear reality of ecstatic satisfaction. Love is the stuff of intimacy. We can never learn intimacy in even the most anointed corporate worship. We discover divine love in the inexplicable freedom of solitary confinement with God. We then bring it without so much as a deliberate thought into the great assembly. It simply cannot stay home.

Prophecy tells us that the testimony of Christ will be injected into every nation of the world before His Kingdom comes. If the words of the prophets are true but the hearts of the prophets are steel, how will they see the Son of Love? He alone leaves the hearer defenseless.

I have talked and talked, yet words still fail me. But if you are a child of God and the unspoken language behind these feeble words is foreign to you, you must seek the love of God. You will surely find it. You are in grave danger without it. You were created for passion. You will find it one way or another.

Doctrines of demons will teach you that you can't really find passion in God. They say you cannot really feel spiritual things. They will offer you substitutes. False Christs. "Watch out that no one deceives you. For many will come in my name" (Matt. 24:5). How many have already come to you? What false Christ has failed to fulfill your cavernous soul? Do not be deceived. It is seduction sent to woo you away from the one thing that is real.

Seek the real—with everything in you. More than life. More than breath. More than health. More than blessing. More than gifts. Ask for love. Not just once. Over and over for the rest of your days, till your voice is hoarse, and with shriveled hand you point to your own aged heart and with one dying word whisper, "More."

CHAPTER 8

SEE-THROUGH LIVES

Believers have never needed one another more than the generations of Christians will who sojourn on planet Earth in the latter days. As depraved as our world is today, can you even imagine what life will be like in one hundred years if Christ tarries? We are foolish and biblically off base if we think the church and individual believers will remain unaffected by ever-increasing wickedness. Beloved, we are *already* affected, which is the reason for this book and many others of similar warning.

Yesterday's war tactics are not going to work today. Today's war tactics are not going to work tomorrow. If we're going to stand firm, we can no longer react. We must pro-act. As the world grows more depraved, the church must grow more alert, more equipped, more sanctified, and more unified "so that you may become blameless and pure, children of God without fault in a crooked and depraved generation, in which you shine like stars in the universe as you hold out the word of life" (Phil. 2:15–16).

As we'll discuss in the following chapter, we cannot cut ourselves off from the world. Christ has temporarily assigned us to minister *in it* and *to it*. Christ is returning for a pure Bride who will be living in the most impure world in human history. Her purity will *not* develop accidentally. As wickedness increases, our only wise recourse is to increase our pursuit of God and godliness all the more. We've got to wake up and get fortified!

One vital method of increasing our fortification is addressed in Hebrews 10:24–25. We'll look at these verses several times in the course of this book because they speak directly to the need for increasing attentiveness as the day of Christ's return draws near.

> And let us consider and give attentive, continu-
> ous care to watching over one another, studying
> how we may stir up (stimulate and incite) to love
> and helpful deeds and noble activities; Not forsak-
> ing or neglecting to assemble together [as
> believers], as is the habit of some people, but
> admonishing—warning, urging and encouraging—
> one another, and all the more faithfully as you see
> the day approaching. (Heb. 10:24–25 AMP)

These verses are not just telling believers to keep going to church! Far more is implied in this reference than filling our place on the pew. Our medals for perfect church attendance will do very little to protect us. We need shields and swords and the guts to help each other get armed. By itself, weekly church attendance won't fortify us against the devil's schemes. Shalca Zulu

I practically grew up in church and on a weekly basis easily attended a minimum of four events, yet I was the poster child for defeat. This Scripture is talking about deliberately involving our-selves with one another for the specified purpose of aiding and abetting each other's victories. *Warning, urging, and encouraging one another.* As the return of Christ draws near, those who isolate themselves from the involvement of the Body of Christ will be at great risk for personal disaster. *Yup. Attend on purpose with purpose*

I believe God's question to Cain will become more and more viable to us as surrounding wickedness grows more threatening. "Where is your brother?" (Gen. 4:9).

Will Cain's reply be ours? "I don't know," he replied. "Am I my brother's keeper?" I think in many ways God's answer to that question is *Yes, as a matter of fact you are.* Particularly as the Day is drawing near.

I have been so reluctant to write this chapter that I saved it as one of the last I wrote. I can't leave the subject matter out because it's too important, but I hesitate to use it because I recognize the potential misapplication. Of course, there will always be those who take Christian messages and even Scripture and distort them to rationalize their own behaviors. My hope is that the busy-bodies who would use this exhortation for license to gossip, finger-point, and meddle are too busy doing their thing to read this book.

I'm hoping against hope that each person who does read this will have the maturity and insight to understand and not mis-appropriate what I'm about to say: *If we're going to get fortified against the devil's schemes in an ever-increasingly wicked world, to some wise extent we're going to have to get into other people's business and let them get into ours.*

There. I said it. Help me, Lord, not to regret it!

Check out parts of Hebrews 10:24–25 again: "And let us con-sider and give attentive, continuous care *to watching over one another* . . . and all the more faithfully as you see the day approaching" (emphasis mine).

Some Christians are so watchful of others that they don't watch over themselves. They see specks in other eyes and miss the planks in their own. That's not the kind of thing the writer of Hebrews is talking about. He's talking specifically about "studying how we may stir up (stimulate and incite)" one another "to love and helpful deeds and noble activities." His exhortation is about love, helpfulness, and nobility between believers. These verses are about encouraging one another and watching out for one another, not bulldozing down appropriate boundaries.

Since you and I and all future believers will need one another *all the more as the day approaches,* we need to grow in our trust-worthiness and in purity of heart and motive. We have a responsibility to one another—which means we have a *responsibility* to become the kinds of persons who can help one another *responsibly*. I'd like to suggest two ways we can help one another more responsibly:

- Develop and practice godly discernment from a broader base.
- Develop and practice deliberate accountability from a narrower base.

We have already established that for those of us who are surrounded by ever-increasing depravity, deception, and satanic seduction, one of our greatest needs is discernment. *Godly* discernment. We can't afford to say it's not one of our spiritual gifts. God instructs us to pray for what is lacking in us. Furthermore, the Book of Proverbs is full of exhortations to seek discernment, prudence, and wisdom.

First Corinthians 14:12 says, "Since you are eager to have spiritual gifts, try to excel in gifts that build up the church." Discernment will be one of those, particularly in the latter days. Discernment does not mean a critical or judgmental spirit. Those are nothing more than fleshly counterfeits.

Embodied in the concept of discernment is the ability to *see through* what may not be completely obvious to the eye. Among other vital empowerments, discernment sees trouble, senses a warning, and cites the need for caution. One rule of thumb we want to establish adamantly is that we can't practice *godly* discernment if we don't walk in the Spirit (Gal. 5). We can't trust what we're sensing in the spirit if we're not filled with the *Holy Spirit*.

In the two bullets on page 136, you will notice that I have "broader base" by the practice of discernment and "narrower base" by the practice of accountability. Let me see if I can explain why. One of the wisest protections you and I can possibly have is an active, deliberately formed small group of people to whom we are accountable. We'll discuss that narrow base in just a moment.

What if I sense something overwhelming in my spirit about a brother or sister in Christ, but that person is not part of my "accountability group"? Do I ignore what I'm sensing because that person's life is really none of my business, or do I go to them? What would I want if the situation were reversed and someone sensed something wrong in me? Would I care about my pride more than I care about avoiding a potential collision with disaster?

The "rules" are far more clear-cut when a brother or sister has fallen into sin, but I'm hoping to help us *avoid* a few plummets! Hebrews 3:13 says, "Encourage one another daily, as long as it is called Today, so that none of you may be hardened by sin's deceitfulness."

So, what do we do if to the best of our understanding we are filled by the Holy Spirit and we sense something is wrong with a fellow believer? What do we do when we fear she (or he) might be falling for a snare of sin's deceitfulness?

First, we'd better spend *serious* time in prayer! Needless to say, we are taking a big risk of offending a brother or sister, especially if we're off base. If God does not seem to release us from our concern, and particularly if we discern a problem the next time we're around the person, God may have an appointment for us.

God may desire that we make a loving approach at an appropriate time just to say we've had him or her on our minds and ask if everything is all right. Then leave the results up to the Holy Spirit. I can't count the times that I've approached a sister in this way and been told that everything was fine . . . only to hear from her several days later.

Whether the problem turned out to be a heavy heart, discouragement, temptation, or a besetting sin, my sister needed encouragement and lots of love. I've needed it, too, and God has never failed to bring someone into my path who discerns when something is wrong. Often God may appoint a person I'd never suspect. You see, sometimes our discernment can be clouded by strong feelings in closer relationships, but it "works" with startling clarity around those with whom we are a little less emotionally *yuple*

involved. Odd, isn't it? That's why discernment can and needs to be exercised in a much broader base.

Let's throw out another hypothetical situation. Let's say I have no hard evidence, but I discern something wrong in a fellow believer or in a relationship between believers. After much prayer, God appoints me discreetly and lovingly to approach the person with concern.

What if my discernment only seems to be confirmed in the encounter but he or she rejects the concern or warning? I've had that very thing happen just recently. My heart broke as I feared impending disaster in a relationship a sister in Christ was developing. I did not go to her until the Holy Spirit seemed to overwhelm me with concern and bring me to a place where I could not remain silent. I went to this precious sister very discreetly and lovingly on two occasions, but both times she assured me the relationship was "safe."

What am I to do? First of all, I hope she's right and I'm completely off target. I'd rather my sister be perfectly fine than me be right. Secondly, I'm just going to have to continue to pray until God releases me, and I must entrust her to her very faithful Father in heaven.

Jude 22–23 says, "Be merciful to those who doubt; snatch others from the fire and save them." Some people won't let themselves be "snatched" from the fire. Tragically, I can think of a few times someone tried to snatch me from a fire, and I thought the person was overreacting. Boy, did I end up getting burned. Thankfully, I can think of other times I received a word of caution and jumped like a maniac from the rising flame.

One thing I believe I can say with confidence and based on personal experience is that we usually "hear" the warning whether or not we "heed" it. Even though I rejected a sound word of warning at a critical time in my life, I was unable to forget it, and God used it later to keep me from being deceived even further by the enemy. Likewise, I don't believe my sweet sister in Christ has forgotten that I came to her in concern. What if God simply uses the warning to give her extra caution in the relationship and all turns out well? So be it!

We are going to need wisdom, spiritual sensitivity, and spiritual *sensibility* like never before as Satan enlarges his seductive attacks against believers. Yes, in some ways we must become our brother's keeper, but if we are not motivated by love and encouragement, we're not moving at the impulse of the Holy Spirit. Witch-hunts or our own Christian version of McCarthyism is out of the question. If we are not motivated by the Spirit through love, God is not the one calling us to get involved in someone else's business. *Oh, God, help us to know the difference and not to use our freedom as a license for sin. We are desperate for the mind of Christ, the heart of Christ, and the direction of Christ.*

A second suggestion for helping one another responsibly involves developing and practicing a narrower base of accountability. If we're going to be fortified against seduction, you and I urgently need a small group of people who we invite to hold us accountable to the pursuit of godliness. Accountability partners mean individuals we invite to *see through* us.

Everyone from the pastor to the church "doorkeeper" needs accountability, but none of us can be forced into it. The structure can be placed around us and the process even demanded of us, but how transparent we are with others will always be a choice. Transparency for the believer is a *wise choice*. Only those who are willing to be vulnerable will experience the protection accountability can bring.

My present purpose in this chapter is not to outline structures for accountability groups. I want rather to encourage you as I've been encouraged to allow several other people of spiritual maturity, godly integrity, and discretion to really know you and hold you accountable to the pursuit and practice of godliness.

Our accountability partners are so important that we want to choose them prayerfully and soberly under the leadership of the Holy Spirit. We may find that the best accountability partners are not necessarily our "best" friends because sometimes we need more objectivity than close friends can provide. Those we ask to hold us accountable should be people we deeply respect and who have proved trustworthy over a length of time. (Beware of instant intimacy with *anyone!* Instant intimacy is one of the leading warning signals of a seduction!)

Although I am very public about *general* confessions of sin, weakness, and fault, God calls me to be far more specific with the handful of people He has placed around me for accountability. I laughed with someone the other day in the ministry office about the fact that we hold each other so accountable, no one can even sneeze around there without someone asking what got in her nose. That's OK with me! I find tremendous comfort and relief in tight accountability. I lived behind a mask for so long that once I got past the painful transition, I began to love the freedom of transparency. I also like the security of knowing that several of those around me have made serious commitments to me, this ministry, and *God* to alert me (and my board of directors if necessary) to things I may be too blind to see. *Particularly things in me.*

Posted plainly in our ministry suite are instructions for staff members and volunteers in the event of any questionable behavior in me. Several staff members and directors on our board as well as my husband and a personal friend know everything there is to know about me. *The good, the bad, and the ugly.* They have open access to question me about absolutely anything. How I thank God for them! Only heaven will prove how they have aided and abetted my pursuit of godliness and my protection from the evil one.

The apostle Paul taught volumes about good accountability partners because he assumed that role with his young churches through his epistles. In fact, our key verse for this book implies several descriptions of the kind of godly accountability we need in the increasing wickedness surrounding us.

> I am jealous of you with a godly jealousy. I promised you to one husband, to Christ, so that I might present you as a pure virgin to him. But I am afraid that just as Eve was deceived by the serpent's cunning, your minds may somehow be led astray from your sincere and pure devotion to Christ. (2 Cor. 11:2–3)

Paul left no doubt in his letter to the Corinthians. He intended to hold them accountable to godliness. He had a *godly jealousy* for their best.

Please notice a critical element in Paul's accountability approach: his desire was their devotion to *Christ*—not their devotion to *him*. God-ordained yokefellows are jealous for us to be God's, not theirs. Godly accountability is never codependency.

Paul demonstrates another wonderful characteristic in a godly accountability partner. He had the ability to recognize and acknowledge strengths in his companions in the faith while still discerning risks. In 2 Corinthians 11:3, Paul commended their sincere and pure devotion to Christ. Who wants an accountability partner who does nothing but point out weaknesses and spout warnings? I don't! I need a little encouragement sometimes, and so do you. Surely *something* is worth commending in us from time to time! If not, we need more than an accountability partner! The last thing Paul wanted was for the Corinthians to lose heart (2 Cor. 4:1). On the other hand, Paul was not blinded to the risks their present weaknesses heightened. He didn't just fret over the fears he had for them. Under the inspiration of the Holy Spirit, he spoke plainly and lovingly. They *heard* whether or not they *heeded*.

See-through lives. That's what we need. Whether we realize it or not, you and I are desperate for people who can see through our lives. With their help, we can begin practicing lives of inside-out veracity that *anybody* can see through. What freedom! What peace! Take it from a former Cover Girl . . . and I don't mean the pretty kind. I mean the kind who writes "Keep Out!" across her forehead in permanent marker and keeps herself covered no matter what the cost. Well, the cost is inestimable. Oh, what joy those days stole from me!

I remember being nineteen years old and sitting in a crowded auditorium at Southwest Texas State University. It was Awards

Night, and the room was electric with excitement. Students, teachers, and parents filled the seats. The time finally came for the emcee to call out the names of twelve college students, six boys and six girls, who had been voted by a student body of nearly sixteen thousand as all-campus favorites. It was one of the most coveted honors at my (rather social) university.

"Beth Green." My stomach jumped into my throat. My parents were so proud they cried. Everybody clapped and hugged me. I stood on the risers with the other eleven campus favorites as the audience gave us a lengthy standing ovation. I smiled and tried to capture the moment as best my handicapped heart could, but the enemy came to steal. I couldn't get over thinking, *But if they really knew me, would they still like me?* That question or one like it haunted me for years, stealing so many moments God meant to be wonderful. Inside, I was full of fear, vastly unhealthy, and prone to poor choices. But I wasn't unlikable. I was *unhealthy.*

Satan would still love to torture me with a low self-esteem. Trust me. Very few people who suffered childhood victimization have naturally healthy self-esteem.

While secluded in the mountains writing this book, I opened a gift my staff had tucked in my suitcase. It was a flip calendar spanning the time I was there, and each day had on it an outdoor scene, a Scripture, and a personalized note for me from one of them. The time they had taken and the affection that filled it was so astonishing to me that I cried like a baby. The tears are stinging in my eyes again just thinking about it!

On the very last day, I flipped the calendar to the final picture. This time it wasn't an outdoor scene. It was a picture of all

144

nine of us. *My friends and me. My precious coworkers in the gospel.* I laughed and bawled at the same time. I sat there before the Lord marveling at the excellence of those He has placed around me, and I heard Him whisper to my spirit, "Look at the kinds of people who love you, Beth. And, yes, they really know you."

They know my past. They know my faults. They know my fears. They know my insecurities. I finally allowed a group of people to see right through me. *And they love me anyway.* Oh, what joy! A joy I will no longer allow the enemy to steal. Somewhere along the way, the Cover Girl broke free. She may not be pretty. But she's real.

The accepting love God has shown me through them, through my husband, and through many others who really know me has given me the courage to stand before thousands and be who I am: A ragamuffin pulled from the pit and saved by the grace of an awesome God. And I am no longer ashamed.

Discernment: the ability to see through the masks.

Accountability: inviting others to see through us.

Both help us *see this faith thing through* with integrity.

CHAPTER 9

WARM HEARTS, WISE HEADS

I n the previous chapter, we highlighted the need for the vital protection of discernment, accountability, and transparency. In a world of increasing deception, wickedness, and seduction, we're realizing that our need for one another is also increasing. God will use the accelerating demands of the latter days to unify the Body of Christ, but each generation is wise to be on the lookout for Satan's ever-increasing counterfeits. For thousands of years Satan has specialized in counterfeiting man's need for closeness and fellowship. Our focus throughout this chapter will be guarding against relational seductions and perhaps a host of other kinds of unhealthy relationships by making sure we are healthy, or what the Bible calls *sanctified through and through.* Keep in mind four important facts to help you avoid making wrong assumptions as we consider this dimension of our study:

1. Seduction does not always involve personal relationships between people. For instance, people can be seduced by false doctrine, money, position, or power and any number of secret addictions to *things. 2. By no means are all unhealthy relationships demonic seduc-tions. 3. Healthy relationships aren't breeding grounds for seductions.* So don't get paranoid and start looking for a demon behind every friend! *4. Relational seduction certainly does not always involve phys-ical or sexual impropriety.* Satan can use relational seduction to pro-mote all kinds of evil, not just those of a sexual nature. He preys upon man's basic bent toward socialization.

In Matthew 24:12, Christ foretold that in the latter days many hearts will grow cold *because of the increase of wickedness.* Christ has called us instead to stand firm to the end and never give in to a coldness of heart. To Christ, loving was living. The last thing you and I are going to allow the enemy to do is talk us into protecting ourselves from relationally induced seduction by shutting our hearts in a stainless steel box. Wouldn't that be just like a bunch of humans to opt for the easy out and detach from people? Disconnection is not an option for followers of Christ. Christ didn't give His life for church doctrine. He gave His life for people. The Word became flesh for the precise purpose of con-necting. Likewise, you and I, believers in Jesus Christ, have been left on this earth for the unapologetic purpose of connecting

- with a lost world through the gospel of Jesus Christ.
- with people in need in the name of Jesus Christ (feeding, clothing, helping).
- with the Body of Christ for the love of Jesus Christ.

In terms of ministry, people are everything to us because they are everything to Christ. Our job is to learn how to be healthy, sanctified connectors. The necessity swells with the reality that a lot of needy and unhealthy folks are out there. Folks who need ministry. Folks whom Jesus loves. Lives that He wants to redeem. We are His physical body meant to flesh out His ministry to the world, and we can't do our jobs properly or safely if we're not spiritually and emotionally healthy.

In Christ's intimate prayer to His Father in John 17, He interceded powerfully not only for His first disciples but also for those who will believe in Him through their message (v. 20). That's you and me and every other believer who has accepted the testimony of Christ's life and gospel as delivered by that first ragamuffin band. John 17:15a and 18 overrule the merest thought we might have of locking ourselves within the church walls as the world around us increases in wickedness. "My prayer is not that you take them out of the world. . . . As you sent me into the world, I have sent them into the world."

We've been sent to the very world the church will probably grow increasingly tempted to avoid. The huge irony is this: we still wouldn't avoid unhealthy relationships because so many of us lack wholeness, having never allowed God to perform His work in us through and through. Here's the shocker: we wouldn't even avoid demonic seductions by shutting out the world and limiting our relationships to those within our church communities. Do you know why? Because so much of it takes place *right there.*

One of the synonyms for the word *schemes* regarding Satan's tactics specifically against Christians in Ephesians 6:11 is *trickery.* One of the tricky elements to a relationship Satan has targeted for seduction is that the union may not be with an unbelieving or apparently worldly individual. If Satan wants to seduce a spiritual person, he's often going to use spiritual bait. We're going to learn something highly important as we seek to seduce-proof our close relationships within the church community: the goal is *godly* relationships, not *spiritual* relationships. You might be interested to know that I have heard from few believers in the last several years who were caught in a relational seduction with those they regarded as unbelievers or even those that at first seemed to be prodigal believers. Of course, those scenarios happen plenty of times, but I thought you could use the eye-opener of my own case studies. I will go a step even further: many of them told me one of the very things that attracted them most was the other person's spirituality. Spirituality does not equal godliness *in either party* nor does being deeply spiritual about Christian things. All sorts of seductions take place in spiritual settings. Seductions among church choir members, church staff, ministers and lay leaders, leaders and laity. Unfortunately, the opportunities are endless, but the point is not to get cynical or suspicious but to get protected and make wise, discerning decisions. Awareness of the possibility is key. In the wonderful book *Spurgeon on Prayer and Spiritual Warfare,* Charles Spurgeon included the following quote by Thomas Spencer:

> The chameleon, when he lies on the grass to catch flies and grasshoppers, takes upon him the color of the grass, as the polypus does the color of the rock under which he lurks, that the fish may boldly come near him without suspicion of danger. In like manner, Satan turns himself into that shape that we least fear, and sets before us such objects of temptation as are most agreeable to our

natures, so he may the sooner draw us into his net;
he sails with every wind, and blows us the way
that we incline ourselves through the weakness of
nature.[1]

I'm anticipating the question as to whether or not those Satan could use readily against another could be Christians at all. You may recall in Matthew 16:23 that Satan used Peter against Christ, and Peter was no doubt a Christian. I'm certainly not implying that all people who claim to be or seem to be Christians *are*. Paul clearly states in the same chapter as our original focal Scripture that "Satan himself masquerades as an angel of light. It is not surprising, then, if his servants masquerade as servants of righteousness" (2 Cor. 11:14–15). I'm simply pointing out the scriptural possibility that Satan can use believers in all sorts of ways if given the opportunity. He simply can't possess them.

One thing we must be warned to avoid at all costs is judging another man's heart. That job is for God and God alone. Judging another man's heart, however, is not the same as discerning that something doesn't seem quite right and considering that we might wisely avoid opening ourselves to an intimate or close relationship in that situation. God looks upon all our hearts, and *ours* must be right before Him even when we're tempted to wonder if someone else's heart is right before Him.

Stop and reflect momentarily on everything we've discussed in this chapter so far concerning the world and the church. Do you see the quandary? As people who desire to seduce-proof our lives, we see that the world is going to get increasingly wicked, yet we've been sent smack into the middle of it. We can't even find a

guaranteed safe haven in our church communities because relational seductions happen there too. What's a person to do? Get
healthy and sanctified right in the middle of all of it and pray for
much of the Body of Christ to get educated and do likewise! We
are not going to find a guaranteed safe place in which to hide. We
are going to have to find safety in Christ, hiding ourselves in
Him, no matter what kind of place surrounds us. Anywhere He
sends us, He is prepared to protect us. We just have to keep ourselves in Him through sanctification.

In the same chapter, John 17, where Christ stated His intention of sending us out into the world, He also prayed that His
own would be one: "May they be brought to complete unity to
let the world know that you sent me and have loved them even
as you have loved me" (v. 23).

We can't become suspicious or phobic toward one another.
The last instruction you would ever get from this book is to start
a witch-hunt within the church communities. If each person concerns himself and herself with personal wholeness and sanctification in Christ, we'll find the protection we need. We'll discern
that there are plenty of people out there in the Body of Christ
who are safe for wonderfully close, godly relationships.

Developing a relationship phobia within the Body of Christ
not only would be a clear violation of Scripture, but what joy and
blessing we would miss! I am so grateful for the dear relationships
God has given me. Without my staff of "iron" women (Prov.
27:17) at Living Proof Ministries, I not only would lose my
sharpness, I couldn't fulfill my calling! In addition to my coworkers, my good friends not only challenge me to press on in
my walk of faith; they make me laugh my head off. In the tape

series *Jesus the One and Only*, I told about a couple of pastors with
whom I served on a leadership team in India. They tricked me
into believing that the people at Nagaland University honor those
who come to address them by having them speak while standing
on a stool. You guessed it. I did it. *For an hour and a half.* When
I wobbled my message to a close, my fellow leaders whom I had
trusted to have some semblance of spiritual maturity, took me to
the side and told me the truth. After beating them half to death
with my Bible and calling their salvation into question, we
laughed until we cried. I am laughing again just telling you about
it. That's one story of a thousand. I've dished out some good,
clean practical jokes myself, but I have more often been the
gullible object.

I have had so much fun with the Body of Christ. I wouldn't
trade my friends in the faith for anything in the world. We cannot allow the enemy to intimidate us into avoiding relationships.
We just want to make sure we develop healthy, God-appointing,
and ever-balancing ones. The way we get started is by becoming
the kind of person we want to find out there. I'm praying that
we're going to learn what those kinds of relationships look like in
the following chapter. Before we do, we still have something vital
to learn from Christ's intercession for us in John 17. Earlier when
I quoted John 17:15a and 18, I purposely left out certain
Scriptures so I could present them to you now. Read John
17:15–18 with nothing missing:

> I do not ask that You will take them out of the
> world, but that You will keep and protect them
> from the evil [one]. They are not of the world

(worldly, belonging to the world), [just] as I am
not of the world.

Sanctify them—purify, consecrate, separate
them for Yourself, make them holy—by the Truth.
Your Word is Truth.

Just as You sent Me into the world, I also have
sent them into the world. (AMP)

We have been sent into this world. To disconnect would be
direct disobedience of purpose. We've also established that Jesus
wants nothing more for His Body than our unification. We must
stay connected. What we need in both these "worlds" is protection from the evil one. Christ already knew that and petitioned
His Father for that very thing. Our means of protection is stated
clearly in the passage: *sanctification*. We can't get away from the
concept, can we? We're terribly vulnerable in our earthly walks
without it. Sanctification is the Holy Spirit's awesome work of
setting us apart—purified and consecrated to God—while we're
still in troubled settings. Even the process of protective sanctification is stated clearly. We are sanctified by the Truth. God's
"word *is* truth" (John 17:17, emphasis mine). We are protected
from the evil one when we start allowing, indeed inviting, the
Word to penetrate us *through and through* with its full power and
authority.

Aren't we doing that already? After all, what are all those sermons and Bible studies about? I cannot overemphasize the
importance of the next few statements. First of all, much of the
Body of Christ exists on very little of the actual Word of God.
Secondly, many of those who get a steady diet of the Word of

God don't deliberately receive it (by applying it) *through and through*. We can get truth into our *heads* without necessarily letting it get through to the inner recesses of our minds, literally changing the entire way we process thoughts. Likewise, we often let the Word get to our *hearts*—even bringing us to tears—but don't invite it to take complete residency and authority over our seat of emotions so we can trust some of the things we feel. Further, we say the Word of God is food for our *souls,* but do we give the Holy Spirit freedom and authority to use it to increasingly transform our entire personalities? Allowing the Holy Spirit to get the Word *through and through* us instead of just *to* us is the kind of thing 2 Corinthians 3:18 is talking about.

> And all of us, as with unveiled face, [because
> we] continued to behold [in the Word of God] as
> in a mirror the glory of the Lord, are constantly
> being transfigured into His very own image in ever
> increasing splendor and from one degree of glory
> to another; [for this comes] from the Lord [Who
> is] the Spirit. (AMP)

Do we really behold as with unveiled faces? No masks? No pretense? Totally unveiled for the purpose of coming to reflect the very image we're beholding? Do we let the Word of God not just get *to* us but get *through and through* us? I want to lovingly suggest that if we are not deliberately asking God to get into every part of our "business," we're probably not practicing the approach that will protect us. Without a doubt, this issue has been the difference between my former approach to the Word of God and my present approach to the Word of God. In the old days, I truly loved the Word and had begun to study it feverishly, but the enemy could still have victory over me because I was unknowingly blocking the power and protection of the Word from parts of my life that I either ignored or denied. He was only getting full reign over what seemed most obvious to this sight-impaired believer. Those old parts of my life weren't presenting me any immediate or obvious problems, so I simply didn't apply the full authority of the Word to them. What a mistake!

I wasn't actively asking God to change the entire way I think, feel, and perceive, dramatically and increasingly transforming me from glory unto glory. Now I'm a maniac about it. Maybe because I scared myself to death. Maybe because I realized Satan could do things I didn't know he could do. And, more than anything, maybe because I finally realized God's Word was meant for a whole lot more than I was allowing. These days I want it to the marrow! I don't want a single inch of my body, soul, or spirit to myself. Sanctify it all, Lord Jesus! It's Yours! I don't want an inch.

That's exactly what the Word of God was meant to do. Take a good look at Hebrews 4:12–16:

> For the Word that God speaks is alive and full
> of power—making it active, operative, energizing
> and effective; it is sharper than any two-edged
> sword, penetrating to the dividing line of the breath
> of life (soul) and [the immortal] spirit, and of joints
> and marrow [of the deepest parts of our nature],
> exposing and sifting and analyzing and judging the
> very thoughts and purposes of the heart.

And not a creature exists that is concealed
from His sight, but all things are open and
exposed, naked and defenseless to the eyes of Him
with Whom we have to do.

Inasmuch then as we have a great High Priest
Who has [already] ascended and passed through
the heavens, Jesus the Son of God, let us hold fast
our confession [of faith in Him],

For we do not have a High Priest Who is
unable to understand and sympathize and have a
fellow feeling with our weaknesses and infirmities
and liability to the assaults of temptation, but One
Who has been tempted in every respect as we are,
yet without sinning.

Let us then fearlessly and confidently and
boldly draw near to the throne of grace—the
throne of God's unmerited favor [to us sinners];
that we may receive mercy [for our failures] and
find grace to help in good time for every need—
appropriate help and well-timed help, coming just
when we need it. (AMP)

The news that everything in and about our lives is naked
and lay bare before God is not meant to terrify His own children or make us feel guilty or condemned. These words are
meant to tell us that—because of Christ's death and ongoing
intercession—the healing, life-giving, wisdom-rendering power
of God's Word reaches every single part of us, even the deepest
parts of our nature. Nothing in us or about us is unaffected by

the Word when we allow God to exercise His wise and protective dominion.

Hebrews 4:12 describes the Word of God as "full of power." One of the ways the original word for "power" was used in extra-biblical Greek was for drugs that were effective in bringing cure.[2] The word was often used as a medical term. Likewise, the Word of God applied to every part of our lives affects us with greater healing and wholeness. We will find grace and help for *every* need. Even those we're embarrassed we have.

Since making my pursuit the absorption of God's Word into every single part of myself, asking that nothing be left untouched, unplowed, and unchanged, Satan has not been able to win a single major victory over my life. I have now practiced this approach for years, and though the enemy has certainly opposed me, annoyed me, and aggravated me, he has not been able to gain a stronghold over me. Whatever you do, don't misunderstand this to be some big accomplishment on my part. None of this has been by might nor by power but by the Spirit of God applying the Word of Truth *through and through*. When I cease to allow Him full freedom, I will undoubtedly return to cycles of defeat.

I relentlessly share what I have learned about victory because I am positive if these practices will work for someone who had as much brokenness and defeat in their past as I did, they will work for anyone. God does not play favorites. All He wants us to do is admit our need and welcome Him thoroughly. I am also compelled to share what I've learned because I believe many Christians are just like I used to be. They are convinced they are allowing the Word to do its sanctifying work simply by a steady diet of sermons and Bible studies. They even love the Word. Still they may have unknowingly practiced such selective application that some places remain inadvertently unprotected. No need to wait until something painful happens. You can change your approach today! Begin aggressively asking God to plow through your precious life with His Word. Don't be scared to do it! Be scared *not* to do it! You're perfectly safe with God.

Begin practicing an open dialogue with Him concerning your past, present, and future. Talk candidly to Him concerning all weaknesses, temptations, and tendencies to sin. Ask Him on an ongoing basis to reveal any area of your life that you may be unknowingly keeping under lock and key from the reaching, healing power of His Word. Approach God as your daily counselor, your soulologist (psyche-ologist) who knows you better than you know yourself. Not only will you find protection, you will discover a level of intimacy with Him unlike anything you've ever experienced. The tears are stinging in my eyes for you just thinking about it!

Let the Word of God sanctify you *through and through!* We've got a world out there that needs the ministry Christ has assigned to us. We've got a Body of believers to love and serve. We don't want to be accidents waiting to happen in either of those important fields. Let's allow God to have His unhindered way with every part of us, neglecting nothing. As He accomplishes His good work, we will grow increasingly low risk for defeat and seduction and increasingly high risk for joy and harvest.

CHAPTER 10

CLEAN TIES

I am a visual learner. Perhaps many of you are as well. This chapter will help us think in concepts. At its conclusion I want us to be able to diagram the kinds of healthy ties that will guard us against relational seduction. Please read the preceding chapter if you haven't already, so you will have a proper foundation for applying what we will now discuss. Again, please keep in mind that not all seductions are relational and not all relational seductions are physical or sexual.

In part 1 we discussed how the Word of God often calls demons "unclean spirits." Those of us who have received Christ Jesus as our personal Savior have received the Holy Spirit into our lives. He literally resides in us. You and I have been made clean by the sanctifying work of the Holy Spirit. He moved into us, bringing His cleanness with Him.

We have seen that Satan attacks believers in spiteful vengeance because God refused to let him be "like the Most High" (Isa. 14:14). Satan knows full well that God wants to present His Son with a pure, spotless, virgin bride, so he's doing everything he can to defile her. What he doesn't seem to "get" is that he cannot touch or taint the Spirit of Christ in us, which is what ultimately gives us our pure standing before God. Still, we want to be sanctified "through and through . . . kept blameless at the coming of our Lord Jesus Christ" (1 Thess. 5:23). Thankfully, the One who calls us is faithful and He will do it (v. 24).

Satan, the ultimate Mr. Unclean, hates that mortal creatures have been made clean through the grace of Calvary and the sanctifying work of the Holy Spirit. If he can't make us unclean, he will at least do everything he can to make us *feel unclean.* He knows that our unclean feelings can eventually cause us to *act* unclean. Social creatures that we are, Satan knows misery loves company and that unclean relationships hasten unclean actions. Simply put, *Satan wickedly yearns for clean people to form unclean ties.*

Therefore, our responsibility and powerful defense is to learn to form *clean ties.* I am intentionally walking through this concept at an elementary pace because I think it is so important. I want it to be very clear.

Please understand a vital key for applying the concept of *clean ties* accurately. By *ties* I mean all close friendships, associations, and relationships. When I use the word *clean,* to receive the greatest amount of protection, I ask you to deliberately translate the word more widely than that which is "opposed to filthy." I ask you to translate the word *clean* as "opposed to messy."

Let me explain why our definition is critical. Many ties aren't clean that don't necessarily fall under the category of filthy. A relationship doesn't have to be "dirty" to be unhealthy and/or seductive. It can simply be messy. For our present purposes, we'll adopt the meaning of the word *messy* as the antithesis of *clean* according to its definitions in *Merriam Webster's Collegiate Dictionary.*

"Messy: Marked by confusion, disorder, or dirt . . . careless, slovenly . . . extremely unpleasant or trying."[1]

As you can see, the word *clean* encompasses a far broader meaning than the opposite of filthy. Most Christians quickly stereotype any kind of sexual sin as dirty, but we can find ourselves in a seductive mess that never gets physical. Let's go ahead and discuss sexual seduction to some degree first. Then we'll broaden our thinking to include other kinds of messy relationships.

In chapter 2 we discussed how powerfully Satan is using sexual seduction. Let's restate that sexual sin *can be* virtually unmatched in its destructive and addictive power. Unhealthy sexuality is an extremely blatant target for seduction. In our previous chapter, we established that not all unhealthy relationships are the specific targets of demonic seduction. I am convinced, however, that every assault on the believer's life to get him or her involved in an extramarital sexual relationship is *seduction*. My grounds for such a categorization is the Book of Proverbs, which labels the tempter to sexual sin a seducer or seductress. (See the seventh chapter of Proverbs for one of the clearest examples.)

Perhaps the only positive thing about sexual seduction is that it can be clearer to recognize than some other forms of relational seduction. We must learn to form "neater" and "cleaner" ties. That picture will become clearer momentarily. Allow me to go ahead and say, however, that an extramarital tie of any kind has lost its "cleanness" and "neatness" the moment *any level of sexuality enters into it.*

Many adults are shocked when they learn that numerous teenagers equate sexual sin solely with the act of (premarital) sexual intercourse. To a staggering number of teens who consider themselves moral and obedient to their parents, anything else goes. In fact, if you are a parent of a young adolescent, you need to be very clear about what you consider the boundaries of appropriate affection for your son's or daughter's relationships. Don't assume they share your same definition of *inappropriate.*

While we say we can't imagine our youth being so foolish, many adults act just as childishly and irresponsibly. Countless adults enter into all sorts of sexual sin through elicit conversation, off-color teasing, flirting, and inappropriate demonstrations of affection. As long as they don't commit fornication, they rationalize that they really haven't done anything wrong.

If we're going to be protected against sexual seduction, we must recognize a radical standard of holiness. Any sign of relating sexually to anyone besides our marriage partner signals a demonic scheme of seduction. I believe that includes any intrusion into the thought life or what the world calls the "fantasy life."

The Word of God uses a very strong command for times when we're tempted to sexual immorality: *flee!* (1 Cor. 6:18). Scripture tells us to run for our lives from sexual sin. Recently I talked with a believer who has been caught in a scheme with a neighbor. If the situation is not diffused immediately, one of them needs to *move.* The same is true of a budding extramarital relationship at work. If it can't be diffused without delay, someone needs to change jobs or, at the very least, departments. Do these sound like radical responses? They are! But that's what God means when He says, "Flee!"

If the believer has already been caught in the web of seduction, he or she may "feel" a diminished power to run. What should that believer do? *Tell someone in godly authority whom he or she can trust!*

Let me give you a prime example. A friend who lives in another city is on the support staff at her church. Satan began to tempt this dear Christian wife and mother with an attraction to one of the ministers with whom she worked. She had all the signs of someone on her way to a full-scale seduction and may have even inadvertently ended up being used as an agent of it in the minister's life. (He had shown no impropriety, and his activity toward her had not exceeded friendliness.)

This godly woman had the wisdom to tell someone she trusted. She admitted her temptation and asked for advice and prayer. Her confidante (not me) gave her both. She called days later with inexpressible joy, saying that since they had talked, she had felt not a hint of attraction nor temptation toward this man. The feelings never returned, and she avoided disaster.

What had happened? Remember, Satan loves a secret! She diffused the scheme when she divulged the secret to someone who in turn helped her through prayer and strict accountability. Hallelujah! She didn't wait until something physical happened. She knew the moment that the relationship took on a hint of sexuality even in her thought processes alone, she was on her way to trouble. You see, *the lines of that tie had already become messy.* She exposed Satan's scheme to the light, and he lost his foothold.

Before we proceed to nonsexual relational seduction, I want to suggest that relating romantically is not the same thing as relating sexually. Godly young couples who are not yet married can relate romantically with a sweet innocence, but even they need to be careful to avoid crossing what can be a fine line of relating sexually. They are prime targets for seductive schemes because their feelings toward one another are so magnetic. They have to be all the more careful not to give the enemy a foothold. He is a shameful opportunist who fights dirty . . . and invisibly. Establishing and paying attention to these kinds of boundaries demands discernment, self-discipline, and enabling by the Holy Spirit, but if young couples are going to be protected, they will have to be wise to the enemy's wiles.

I am no more comfortable talking about this subject matter than you may be reading it, but timidity and lack of clarity won't help us here. Satan so hopes the church won't have guts enough to deal with issues like these. Let's prove him wrong. In Hosea 4:6 the Lord says, "My people are destroyed from lack of knowledge." The Word of God has much to say about Satan's schemes against us. God never hedges from difficult subject matter like this one. The Holy Spirit applies knowledge to us as power.

Satan would do anything to counterfeit the gift of sexuality God gave to a man and wife. Nothing is any "cleaner." Let's guard the precious gift we've been given. Remember, an extramarital tie of any kind has lost its "cleanness" and "neatness" the moment *any level of sexuality enters into it.*

Now let's consider some examples of nonsexual relational seduction. In part 1, I told you about my dear friend who along with her husband was caught in the powerful seduction of a religious cult. They were very active Christians who were enticed by a church that professed to practices very close to those of the early church in the Book of Acts. In actuality very few of their practices ended up imitating the early church—with the convenient exception of pooled finances. They did not realize how far they were veering from the Word into man-induced legalism and bondage because the leaders interpreted the Scripture for them. They were *not* encouraged to study the Bible for themselves. Are you beginning to recognize the signs? They lost the active protection of the ongoing sanctification of God's truth.

In the end, this family was seduced into losing practically everything they had except their salvation and one another. My friend is one of the least gullible people I know. She testifies that this cult had a terrifying seductive power to control the mind and blind the eyes. Keep in mind that any kind of mind manipulation that draws a believer away from his or her *wholehearted, sincere, and pure devotion to Christ* qualifies as a demonic seduction according to 2 Corinthians 11:2–3.

For our present subject matter, pay particular attention to the following dimension of Satan's scheme. My friend said that the hardest part of the cult to walk away from was the closeness of the members to *one another*. Their lives were extremely intertwined. They did everything together and knew virtually everything about one another.

The separation was "bloody" because they were all skintight. Defectors couldn't simply clip the ties and walk away. They had to tear themselves away. They were not bound in the Spirit. They were bound in their Spirit-mimicking flesh. Dependency counterfeited genuine unity. Their ties were not sexual, but they were *messy*. There's our key word.

I'll address one more example of nonsexual relational seduction in hopes that you'll have enough information to recognize the messy lines that put relationships at risk. Throughout part 1, we referenced two primary texts: (1) 2 Corinthians 11:2–3, where we are warned that a *wholehearted, sincere, and pure* devotee to Christ can be seduced by the serpent and (2) Matthew 24, where Christ foretold the increasing deception and wickedness of the latter days. Not coincidentally, both chapters warn against *false Christs*.

In Matthew 24:4–5, Jesus answered, "Watch out that no one deceives you. For many will come in my name, claiming, 'I am the Christ,' and will deceive many."

In 2 Corinthians 11:4–6, the apostle Paul said, "If someone comes to you and preaches a Jesus other than the Jesus we preached, or if you receive a different spirit from the one you received, or a different gospel from the one you accepted, you put up with it easily enough."

In the Matthew example, Christ spoke directly to the false declarations of those who will come claiming to be Him. In the example in 2 Corinthians, Paul implied that if the Jesus others preach doesn't sound like the Jesus he preached, it's not the same Jesus! Both of these brands of impostors are fairly outward and obvious examples of false "Christs." I'd like to submit to you that Satan can also seduce us with a far subtler kind of false Christ.

Anyone who becomes a "Christ" to us constitutes an unhealthy and ungodly tie no matter how spiritual he or she may be. Whether or not the person intentionally solicits dependency and devotion, Satan's scheme is to subtly transfer the deep devotion the believer has felt to Christ to a mortal instead.

The wrongs on both sides of the earthly relationship are monumental. Any relationship in which we begin to emotionally attribute some of the biblically specified activities of Christ to a person is not only an unhealthy tie; it is a mess. God will not share His glory with another. He will never bless nor eventually even tolerate someone becoming a savior to us.

Years ago I heard an acronym for EASTER that I've never forgotten and have shared often: Every Alternative Savior Takes

Cute and true

Early Retirement! Have you discovered any truth in that state-ment? I have. False christs are false deliverers, false comforters, false forgivers, false providers, and false healers. Their works can-not be sustained and their fruit eventually rots. Christ alone is our salvation. All other christs are seductions.

I promised that we would have a way to visualize and even dia-gram clean ties. For the sake of contrast, I also want to diagram unclean ties so we'll always be able to picture the difference. Do you remember when I listed the common claims of the seduced in part 1? I pointed out that many who were caught in relational seductions, whether sexual or nonsexual, used the word *web* to describe them. I found the repetitive terminology intriguing since those who used it were unrelated to one another and unaware that others had used the same word for seductive ties. The primary translations of Scripture use the word *web* two different times.

- Job 8:13–14 says, "Such is the destiny of all who forget God; so perishes the hope of the godless. What he trusts in is frag-ile; what he relies on is a spider's web."
- Isaiah 59:1–5 says, "Surely the arm of the LORD is not too short to save, nor his ear too dull to hear. But your iniquities have separated you from your God; your sins have hidden his face from you, so that he will not hear. For your hands are stained with blood, your fingers with guilt. Your lips have spoken lies, and your tongue mutters wicked things. No one calls for justice; no one pleads his case with integrity. They rely on empty arguments and speak lies; they conceive trouble and give birth to evil. They hatch the eggs of vipers and spin a spider's web."

Job 8 speaks of those who forget God somewhat like the one who transfers his or her devotion to a false Christ. Surely *what he trusts in is fragile; what he relies on is a spider's web.*

Isaiah 59 speaks of the unrepentant whose fingers are stained with guilt and whose lips speak lies and wicked things. They conceive trouble. They spin a spider's web.

Both visuals ascribe responsibility to those who trust in a web and those who spin a web. Christ can and will destroy such a web, but things can sure get sticky in the meantime. Webs don't make clean relationships, and sometimes a person can still be pulling the sticky stuff off long after the relationship has ended. Freedom begins with the full admission of bondage and sin, shirking no rightful responsibility. Wisdom comes from recognizing both how webs are spun and how to avoid them.

The New Testament does not use the word *web* in any of the four primary translations, but Hebrews 12:1–2 offers some great visuals we can add to our diagrams:

> Therefore then, since we are surrounded by so
> great a cloud of witnesses [who have borne testi-
> mony of the Truth], let us strip off and throw aside
> every encumbrance—unnecessary weight—and
> that sin which so readily (deftly and cleverly) clings
> to and entangles us, and let us run with patient
> endurance and steady and active persistence the
> appointed course of the race that is set before us,
>
> Looking away [from all that will distract] to
> Jesus, Who is the Leader and the Source of our
> faith [giving the first incentive for our belief] and

is also its Finisher, [bringing it to maturity and
perfection]. He, for the joy [of obtaining the prize]
that was set before Him, endured the cross, despis-
ing and ignoring the shame, and is now seated at
the right hand of the throne of God. (AMP)

Hebrews 12:1 says that sin "entangles us." Likewise, I believe
we can draw the application that *sinful* relationships are *entan-
gling* relationships. In this chapter we discussed sexually relational
seductions and then two examples of nonsexual relational seductions. All three examples had messy ties as opposed to the clean
ties that protect the believer from seduction. All of them formed
sinful entanglements. Whether we call it a web or an entangle-
ment, the relationship lacks the clean and uncomplicated lines of
godliness, as you can see in the diagram.

How can we keep our relational ties healthy and clean? Keep Christ between them! Next I've used a diagram of the cross to represent Christ, the one and only Savior, standing between every relationship. Notice how the lines drawn by the cross still connect individuals to one another. We've already established that we would be in clear violation of Scripture to cease connecting to others. If we'll begin imagining the cross between us and each of the parties to whom we're in close relationship, we would have a constant reminder of our need to ask God to crucify any harmful "flesh" that rises up in our relationships. We'd also find such peace in the simplicity of the clean lines.

Notice that the horizontal line of the cross keeps the parties connected, but the vertical line respects God-given boundaries drawn between the two. The Word of God is full of directives

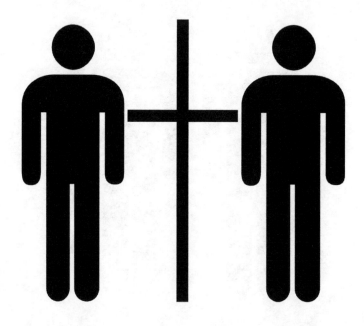

about proper boundaries for believers. We've mentioned three of those in this chapter: lines drawn between unmarried people in any realm of sexual relationship, lines drawn to avoid unhealthy dependency on one another, and lines drawn from allowing anyone to become a false christ to us. Certainly, Scripture cites many others, such as avoiding unequally *yoking* with unbelievers, but I think you have the general idea.

I love the idea of imagining the cross between my closest relationships and me because the representation means so much. Take a moment and think through your closest relationships. Do you have both the vertical and the horizontal lines that the cross represents? How do our relationships match up to the diagram? We are imperfect people and we will always be challenged by imperfect relationships, but I think the lines of the cross between us can offer a plumb line that can become a constant goal.

Finally, let's address an obvious question. What if *we're* willing to respect clean lines in our relationships, but others in the relationship are not? Then they can tangle with the cross! Take a look at the final diagram on the next page. We can't change anyone else. For crying out loud, we can't even change *ourselves!* But we can allow *God* to change us. Our responsibility is to allow God to make each of us healthy, whole connectors and to have the courage to put some distance between any relationship that is a seduction waiting to happen.

You and I need to obey God. When we do, the consequences of our obedience become God's problem and not ours. Others threatened by the change may think they are tangling with us, but as we determine to allow God to manage

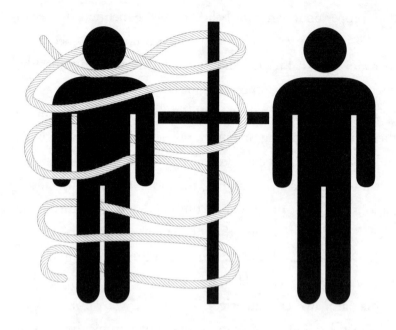

our relationships, we leave Christ to tangle with them instead of us. And, guess what, beloved? He can handle them. No amount of ties can bind *Him*. That's not true of any of the rest of us. Give *Him* the ropes.

CHAPTER 11

STRONG WALLS AND
SECRET PLACES

All this stuff about seduction is really important, but I don't mind telling you, I've got another problem that needs some attention. Keith and I need a new fence. That's all there is to it. Why can't things just *stay fixed?* We replaced the fence not long after we moved into the house. OK, so it's been nearly twenty years, but it seems like yesterday.

Who in the world wants to spend money on a new fence? How boring! Not to mention expensive! If we're going to spend several thousand dollars, I either want to wear it, drive it, sit on it, or eat it for crying out loud! I can't wear a fence. I can't drive a fence. I can't eat a fence. And God sure won't let me sit on a fence. Been there. Tried that. Humpty Dumpty bit the dust.

Anyway, it's not fair. A huge part of our fence problem is coming from the neighbor directly behind us. They innocently planted a small line of trees right against the fence many years ago. Now those trees are about twelve feet tall. Inch by inch the roots have grown in under our fence and into our yard until the uneven ground has completely unearthed the fence posts. The branches that years ago were only twigs have now strengthened until they have dislodged the sturdy nails and pushed the slats right off the horizontal posts.

When the slats started falling, we had no idea what had happened. We thought maybe the old fence was rotting. We had no idea that the trees on the other side that were once nothing but little bushes had overgrown into our yard. They grew so gradually, we didn't notice until the slats of the fence were falling, one right after the other.

Keith and I are not about to march around to our neighbors and say, "Look what your trees are doing to our fence!" That's just not us. We're taking responsibility for our own problem. It's time to realign and rebuild.

Our predicament certainly could be worse. Keith pitched me a magazine the other day and pointed to an article he said I must read. As I did, my eyes grew big as saucers. Another person's fence fell down too. What complicated her situation somewhat is that her property was next to a small wildlife park. Both neighbors had quite a lot of acreage, and she raised miniature horses while her neighbor boasted a variety of "exotic" animals. How did she realize part of her fence was down? One day she looked up and a male lion was tearing her favorite horse to shreds for lunch. True story.

Tragically, we often don't realize part of our fence is down until Satan, the roaring lion, is devouring something precious to us *right on our own property.* Mind you, the devil has no right to be on our property, but all he needs for a written invitation is a weak spot in the fence.

What happened to the Moores' fence is exactly what happens in many of our lives when the enemy gains ground that *does not belong to him.* At some point prior to his complete intrusion into our lives, he laid groundwork. Like our neighbors' trees, this groundwork is often so subtle and seems so harmless that we give it very little notice. Inch by inch, the enemy grows something powerful right on the edge of our fence.

We begin to see a few little hints of weakness in the boundary here and there, but with our busy lives we often pay little attention. Here's the big one: we reason that, after all, nothing disastrous has happened before. Listen carefully, never assume that just because a smaller problem hasn't exploded into a bigger problem *before,* it's never going to. Wrong. That's exactly what the enemy wants us to think. Don't ever forget what a schemer he is. He loves nothing better than supplying a false sense of security. —Lies! One day when we least expect it, we look up and the lion is in the yard and our "pet" is being torn to shreds. Oh, I pray that God will expose every bit of false security we have!

Let me give you a few examples coming from actual testimonies I've heard. A Christian churchgoing man views what he calls "light pornography." He keeps a stack of it in his bathroom. No big deal. "It's not the bad stuff." His wife doesn't like it, but he's done it since college. They've been married for years, and he has never been (physically) unfaithful. It "just hasn't caused him a problem." He's maintained his sport just fine. Then one day, the rules change. The lion is in the yard. *False security. Things didn't stay the same.*

A teenage girl who has struggled with homosexual tendencies through high school wants to be different and *free* from guilt more than anything in the world. She attends a youth rally. The speaker hits hard on the sin of homosexuality. She feels convicted and devastated by her sin. She walks the aisle and receives Christ. She vows never to return to her former practices.

This girl determines to do her best to forget. That's right. She'll just put her past behind her and never think about it again. She promises to be "normal," and since being "normal" must mean being "married," she marries as quickly as she can. She struggles, but who doesn't? The problem is confined to her imagination, and no one knows she has the least thought about her past. She hates it. She hates herself, but she doesn't know how to fix it. She just tries to be as good as she can. She gets involved at church and does everything she can to stay busy. Then one day a woman joins her prayer group. Not just any woman. A woman in active bondage to homosexual sin. The rules change. The problem once confined to the mind has weakened the nails on several slats of the fence. She looks up and the lion is in the yard. *False security. Things don't stay the same.*

A ministry bookkeeper borrows and pays back the bank account for a matter of years. No one knows. Only she does the books. She pays it back anyway. *Eventually.* She's gotten a little sloppy lately. She's let the books get a tad behind. She'll get caught up, though. Money has gotten tight at home. She has a few outstanding debts, but goodness knows the ministry has plenty of money. They'll never even miss it. It's not a big deal. It's gone on for years. Nothing has happened. It's not fair. Her husband left her with two teenagers, and he refuses to pay child support. She just needs a little help until the courts get the whole mess straightened out. No one cares. No one knows. She'll pay it back before anyone figures it out. She's done it before. Then one day, the rules change. The lion is in the yard. *False security. Things didn't stay the same.*

In every example, Satan first laid groundwork. He subtly planted something that appears small, as close to the fence line as possible. Over the course of time, the roots and branches strengthen, and the wall begins to dislodge. The lion gets in the yard, and often by the time we look up, he's devouring something precious. *Relationships, integrity, the respect of our children, our finances, our security, our own self-respect, etc.* And all because we didn't deal with the damage to our fence.

I want to share a visual with you that God gave me based on the Old Testament temple. It has been a tremendous help to me, and I pray that it will be to you too. My hope is that we may simplify something that can be very complex into more manageable terms. Take a look at the diagram below.

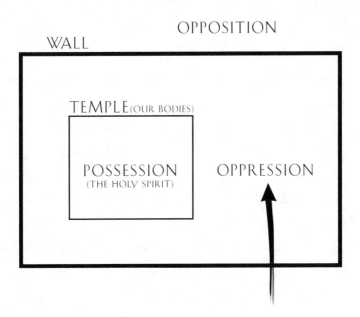

To me the temple is a perfect illustration for a believer's life because the Word of God tells us that since the cross and Pentecost, the Spirit of God dwells in believers. First Corinthians 6:19 says, "Do you not know that your body is a temple of the Holy Spirit, who is in you, whom you have received from God?"

Notice on your diagram that the word *possession* appears *inside* the temple structure. You and I, believers in Christ, are represented by the temple structure itself. In fact, the verse just told us that our actual bodies are the temples of the Holy Spirit. When we received Christ as our Savior, the Holy Spirit took up immediate residence in us.

Romans 8:9 says, "If anyone does not have the Spirit of Christ, he does not belong to Christ." In other words, whether or not you realized what was taking place spiritually, if you deliberately received Christ Jesus as your personal Savior, at that very moment His Spirit moved right into your physical body and now dwells within you.

Once God deposits the Spirit of Christ into our bodies, I believe Scripture teaches that we are sealed and shut tight until we see Christ face-to-face and our redemption is completed in heaven. I believe with all my heart that the Holy Spirit doesn't depart from a believer and no other spirit can enter us.

Ephesians 1:13 tell us that "having believed, you were marked in him with a seal, the promised Holy Spirit." This seal is not just a mark of ownership or a stamp with God's name on it. I believe it is both of those things and more. Paul drew his terminology from the society of his day. Any document of the king or under his authority was marked with a seal. When the king authorized a document or enclosure, his royal insignia was stamped in the warm liquid of wax or precious metal, and it would quickly harden into a seal. The seal could be opened only by the one to whom it was sent or under the direct authority of the king.

God, the King of heaven and earth, has secured you and me so that He can present us as a bride for His Son. Nothing and no one on this earth *or in the heavenlies* has the authority or power to break the seal. We are saved for Christ alone, and on the day of our complete and perfect redemption, face-to-face with Jesus, we will be safe in the hands of the One to whom we've been sent. Until then, nothing gets "in" and nothing gets "out." The reason why we sense the activity of the Holy Spirit differently at times and may even feel that He is no longer in residence is implied further in the same letter.

> And do not grieve the Holy Spirit of God (do
> not offend, or vex, or sadden Him), by Whom
> you were sealed (marked, branded as God's own,
> secured) for the day of redemption—of final deliv-
> erance through Christ from evil and the conse-
> quences of sin. (Eph. 4:30 AMP)

We quench or grieve the Holy Spirit by refusing His authority over us. In other words, by choosing not to yield to Him. He therefore retreats His activity and fullness in us, sometimes even to the point that we may not sense His presence. Still, I do not believe He departs us. *Neither does He lie dormant.* If the Spirit of Christ is in us, we can't just continue on in sin. The absence of both His activity and the *feeling* of His presence will eventually create such a void—or such *havoc*—that we will no longer be able to bear it.

Now let's study the other components in the diagram. We've already paralleled the temple itself to our bodies as believers in Christ. We are possessed by the precious Holy Spirit of God, and no other spirit can possess us. You can also see ground around the temple structure and a wall. On the outside of the wall you will see the word *opposition*. Opposition is a normal part of our existence while occupying these mortal bodies on this earth.

The most victorious, Spirit-filled believers on earth face challenge continually by all sorts of satanic opposition, whether or not they recognize Satan as the source. Ephesians 6:12 clearly says "our struggle is not against flesh and blood, but against the rulers, against the authorities, against the powers of this dark world and against the spiritual forces of evil in the heavenly realms." When we practice victorious lives and allow the sanctifying work of the Holy Spirit to permeate *through and through* every part of our lives, as a rule (though God can make any exception He chooses) Satan is limited to the outside of that wall and can work only through opposition.

Don't downplay how powerful opposition can be, however! Opposition is anything that opposes (1) us, (2) the work God desires to do in us, and (3) the work God desires to do *through* us. Opposition may not even appear oppositional! It may be something that feeds our fleshly pride but opposes everything about who we are in Christ.

Whatever the form of opposition, you can bet Satan is going to plant something powerful as close to our fence line (or wall) as he possibly can. He's hoping to be subtle and gradual enough that we won't become alarmed. He's also hoping to press so hard against that fence that unknown to us, slats start weakening. If he can somehow get a root to grow in under the wall, he is ecstatic.

Satan cannot get inside our temples, so the closest he can get is inside the wall. What does the wall or the fence line represent to you and me? God's will and obedient lives form that perimeter. We gave this kind of life a name in an earlier chapter: *blamelessness.* We can live in a state of being where we are not sinning willfully, and no sin has dominion over us.

How does Satan get inside the wall or fence line? He puts pressure on the outside, hoping to get a reaction or some sort of cooperation from the inside. All he needs is one little piece of the fence or wall to crumble, and the lion's in the yard. I believe Satan ordinarily puts pressure on the wall or fence by raising either *temptation* or *turmoil.* One or the other can eventually lead to both.

Let's talk about *temptation* first: Satan can put pressure on the fence (or wall) by raising temptation right at the fence line. Remember when we talked about the importance of being happy and satisfied in our faith? If we don't take Christ up on the fullness of joy and satisfaction *within* our walls, we are still subject to longing glances at life *outside our walls.*

Too often we live our Christian lives strictly sacrificially, just waiting for heaven where we'll finally be rewarded. All the "fun" appears to be outside the walls, and we secretly yearn for something to awaken our souls. We become an accident waiting to happen. The enemy is deceiving us! Where we are concerned, the grass is *never* greener on the other side. It's nothing but artificial coloring.

The fullest portion of God's presence that mortals can experience is *inside those walls.* As the psalmist said, "You have made known to me the path of life; / you will fill me with joy in your presence" (Ps. 16:11). Many believers never discover the fullness of joy and the lavish sacred romance within those walls. They keep their religious rules and try to be good while, secretly, satisfaction still eludes them. The secret longing weakens the fence. Since it has remained standing for so long, they trust in a false security. One day the rules change, a portion of the wall crumbles, and the lion is in the yard.

What about *turmoil?*

I can speak personally to this one because the enemy used it so effectively in my life. Certainly he has also weakened my wall through temptation, but one of his most powerful schemes against me came through raising turmoil at my fence line. He knew I was an abuse victim whether or not I had ever faced the fact. He raised all sorts of things at the fence line that quickened emotional reactions in me.

Many of the things he raised at the fence line were nothing but lies, but I was too inexperienced to recognize the deception. *Had* I allowed God to permeate my life with His sanctifying Holy Spirit and heal me *through and through,* Satan couldn't have evoked such an inside response from me. I cooperated with the devil because I had not completely cooperated with God.

In my pity-party days, I bawled, "But I didn't know any better! That's not fair!" First of all, we better get a clue. Life isn't fair. Not from any direction. I live in the inconceivable grace of God every day of my life. That's not fair either. Second, God has given us His Word and holds us responsible for knowing what is in it.

God knew good and well I hadn't faced my past and that I didn't have an idea of what Satan could do with it.

God tried to teach me easier ways. Since I didn't learn my badly needed lessons from His Word and easier methods, He found another tool: *the devil himself.* Satan did everything he could at that fence line to get a reaction from me on the inside of that temple. Why did God let him? He didn't just let him. He *used* him. Allowing Satan to call the victim buried within me to the surface became such a teaching tool in the hand of God that I could not ignore it. Nor will I ever forget it.

Proverbs 25:28 says, "Like a city whose walls are broken down / is a man who lacks self-control." *Self-control* is an interesting term. After a list of eight more understandable qualities of the fruit of the Spirit—*love, joy, peace, patience, kindness, goodness, faithfulness, gentleness*—comes a word that almost seems out of place. What does *self*-control have to do with the Spirit? Only *self* can decide who's in *control.* When *self* grants *control* to the Holy Spirit and we live within the boundaries of God's will for our lives, our wall stands firm and Satan must work from more of a distance. He is limited to opposition rather than outright oppression.

Satan hopes to raise such a powerful opposition at the fence line that we lose self-control. In other words, *self* rejects the control of the Holy Spirit and we give way to things like *anger, bitterness, rage, lust, greed, ambition,* or *despair.*

I suggested in part 1 that when Satan targets those with *wholehearted, sincere, and pure devotion to Christ,* he often preys on weakness rather than sin. He looks for things he can raise at the fence line that will awaken our weaknesses and become catalysts for sin. I am reminded of Charles Spurgeon's words: "You may conceal your infirmity, even from your dearest friend, but you will not conceal it from your worst enemy."[1]

Whether Satan targets weakness or sin makes little difference to him if he can cause us to temporarily reject the authority and sanctifying power of the Holy Spirit controlling self. If he can accomplish his goal, just one little area of the wall tumbles down. Sometimes nothing happens right away. Satan often waits to wreak havoc while establishing a sense of false security. Then the rules change. We look up and the lion is in the yard.

Again, Satan cannot enter the temple, but when *self* starts rejecting the control of the Holy Spirit, a portion of the wall tumbles down, and Satan can move from a position of opposition to *oppression*. Check the diagram on page 179 for the word *oppression*.

Once Satan gets inside that wall, the ball game changes dramatically. Oppression is *hardball*. Though the range can vary, oppression is the closest Satan or his demons can get to a believer. The closer proximity of enemy attack can make the assault almost overwhelming. Satan's voice, silent only to our earthly senses, can scream so loudly that the oppressed think they can't hear the voice of God.

I even think it's possible for some people to feel "possessed" by a demon when in reality they are terribly "oppressed." Perhaps demonic oppression can be so powerfully "on" a person that it can feel "in" the person.

Instead of bowing to God, thereby submitting to His unparalleled authority, the oppressed often *bow to the oppression*. They inadvertently bow to their enemy. Satan assumes rights over us he doesn't even have. On our own, he is light years out of our league.

Satan is most assuredly a "powerful enemy" and a "foe too strong" *for me* (Ps. 18:17). But he is under Christ's feet. Relief comes only when we cry out with everything in us for Christ to come and take total control, withholding nothing from Him. *Complete submission.* In all probability we need to submit some things that thus far have gone unnoticed by us or that we have ignored. The full authority of Christ reigning *over* us and *through and through* us is exactly what diffuses the power of the oppressor.

I have become increasingly convinced that we, the Body of Christ, are tragically amiss in exercising our rights as Abba's children. The lion has no right to be in our yard. How does he get there? He stands at the fence line doing everything he can to get a rise out of us. Instead, "Let God arise, let his enemies be scattered: let them also that hate him flee before him" (Ps. 68:1 KJV).

Remember, Satan moves from a more bearable distance of *opposition* to a far less bearable position of *oppression* only by invitation. What is his invitation? One broken place in our fence can say, "Come right on in my yard." Wise we are when we become frequent surveyors of our fence lines.

Where does seduction fit into all of this? Let's put it this way. In our war with demonic powers and principalities, if (relatively speaking) opposition is a game of *softball,* then oppression is *hardball.* And if oppression is hardball, seduction is *curveball.*

Seduction is a form of oppression, of course, but it's a very sly scheme intended to catch us off guard, pitched with mind-boggling velocity from a direction we were not expecting. Seduction means the demonic trickery of a professional liar. If you'll allow me to put it this way, seduction is Satan at his *best.* He's looking for the trickiest means of getting inside our walls, and I doubt he considers anything a greater accomplishment than the broken wall of a devout believer.

God is a big believer in walls. I believe the need for boundaries or walls came with the entrance of the serpent onto the property of God's children. God the Father threw a wall or boundary around the Garden of Eden by the flaming sword of an angel. Later, He instructed the Israelites to build a portable wall around the Old Testament tabernacle. Likewise, the temple had a wall around it, as did the city of Jerusalem. Not coincidentally, even the heavenly Jerusalem described in Revelation 21 has a wall around it (Rev. 21:12–21).

God reserves the right to say what gets to enter the gates and what does not. Revelation 21 concludes with these words: "Nothing impure will ever enter it, nor will anyone who does what is shameful or deceitful, but only those whose names are written in the Lamb's book of life." We are so wise to establish biblical boundaries concerning the deliberate things we want to keep within our walls and keep *out* of our walls.

Oh, how I pray that through the chapters of this book we are learning how to become far more intentional in guarding against the destruction of the enemy. When we establish sturdy walls, we don't have to live in fear. We just let the walls do their jobs. Don't ever forget that Satan can't get in from the outside without an invitation from the inside. Now we're about to consider a powerful way he gains access.

Returning once again to our diagram, I want you to see another parallel with me drawn from Old Testament Scripture that I find nothing less than startling. Read and meditate on every word coming from the eighth chapter of Ezekiel.

In the sixth year, in the sixth month on the fifth day, while I was sitting in my house and the elders of Judah were sitting before me, the hand of the Sovereign LORD came upon me there. I looked, and I saw a figure like that of a man. From what appeared to be his waist down he was like fire, and from there up his appearance was as bright as glowing metal. He stretched out what looked like a hand and took me by the hair of my head. *[Author's comment: I feel like God has taken me by the hair of the head on occasion myself. Anybody else?]* The Spirit lifted me up between earth and heaven and in visions of God he took me to Jerusalem, to the entrance to the north gate of the inner court, where the idol that provokes to jealousy stood. And there before me was the glory of the God of Israel, as in the vision I had seen in the plain.

Then he said to me, "Son of man, look toward the north." So I looked, and in the entrance north of the gate of the altar I saw this idol of jealousy.

And he said to me, "Son of man, do you see what they are doing—the utterly detestable things the house of Israel is doing here, things that will drive me far from my sanctuary? But you will see things that are even more detestable."

Then he brought me to the entrance to the court. I looked, and I saw a hole in the wall. He said to me, "Son of man, now dig into the wall."

So I dug into the wall and saw a doorway there.

And he said to me, "Go in and see the wicked and detestable things they are doing here." So I went in and looked, . . .

"He said to me, "Son of man, have you seen what the elders of the house of Israel are doing in the darkness, each at the shrine of his own idol? They say, 'The Lord does not see us;'. . ." (Ezek. 8:1–10, 12)

Ezekiel 8:7 tells us that Ezekiel was taken *to the entrance to the court*. The following parallel is not a perfect fit in our temple illustration, but I believe it is worthy of our considerations. I looked in several commentaries, and all the commentators I checked agree that this "court" is most likely referring to the *inner court* of the temple. In the parallel that you and I are drawing, the temple structure is our "self," and the "Holy Place" might be considered the actual Spirit of God dwelling within us.

I'd like to suggest that the inner court could represent what is private to us without necessarily being sacred. In other words, the *secret places*. The most secret chamber of our personal lives that we might consider outside the *sacred* could be the *mind*. Many of us may not be committing grievous sins with our bodies (yet!), but we are entertaining them in the recesses of our minds.

When David the psalmist spoke about the inner parts (Ps. 51:6), he referred to the secret places of the mind and heart (or emotions). After his headlong dive into a pit of sin, he realized how much he needed "truth in the inner parts" and "wisdom in the inmost places." We kid ourselves into thinking that sin is safe in the secret places. *I've hearing/reading this in the last weeks-trng April 27 - may 2 08. !!!*

For the believer, I am convinced the mind is often the last inner chamber we allow God to sanctify. One reason is because it is a never-ending challenge to keep clean, and we sometimes adopt the attitude, "Why bother?" Oh, beloved, we must bother because the mind is the biggest battlefield we have on which our spiritual battles are fought. Even our feelings eventually bow down to our thoughts. *Speak Truth*

People continually say, "I can't change the way I feel." But, beloved, if we change the way we *think,* before long our thoughts *Yes!* change the way we *feel.* All sin begins in the mind, and untold secret sin is allowed to flourish there. But not without effect. Sooner or later.

Earlier in the chapter on love, I suggested that one of the most powerful doctrines of demons is the false (often unspoken) belief among many Christians that love for God doesn't *feel.* Another equally powerful demonic doctrine is that minds cannot be clean.

We hear statistics concerning how many impure or negative thoughts go through the typical mind in a sixty-second period, and we buy that standard as an immutable truth. The redeemed of God who are inhabited by the very Spirit of Jesus Christ weren't bought by His blood to be *typical.* No, we can't be perfect or sinless, nor can we find some legalistic means of controlling every thought we have. But can God clean up our negative or impure minds? You bet He can! Furthermore, if we don't let Him, our minds will taint our hearts and ultimately affect our actions. Remember how the apostle Paul said the serpent could get to those with *wholehearted, sincere, and pure devotion to Christ*? By seducing and corrupting their *minds!* (2 Cor. 11:2–3).

As we conclude this portion of the book on how to fortify ourselves against seduction, so much of our work will be in vain if we don't let God sanctify us *through and through*—all the way to the inner court of our *minds*. What are we doing behind the hole in the wall? In the secret places of the mind? In the darkness? What are our idols right there in the inner chambers? Those perhaps no one else knows about?

Dear one, is there a mess behind that hole in the wall? Would you practically die if suddenly your thoughts were somehow exposed to the public? We've all been there. But we don't all have to stay there.

Having our minds sanctified is an ongoing, lifelong process, but absolutely nothing will have a greater harvest in your life. So many people try to get hold of their emotions, but they don't realize the emotions are usually regulated by the *mind*. If we don't start thinking differently, we will never feel differently.

How does the process begin? When I was a little girl, the only illumination in our tiny, dark closets were bare lightbulbs from which a thin chain hung. Step into that dark closet, beloved. Reach up and pull that chain. Let the light of God's presence come into that place. You might say, "But I'll be humiliated to have Him in there!" Dear friend, He's looking right through the hole in the wall. He already knows. He is waiting for you to invite Him in so He can help you sort through the mess and start cleaning it up for you. You *cannot* clean up habitually negative or impure thoughts by yourself.

God *loves* you with an unfailing love. You cannot diminish His love with impure or negative thoughts, but you can diminish your awareness and enjoyment of His love. Trust Him to go behind that hole in the wall, or you'll never be free!

In Mark 12:28–30, when Christ answered the question, "Of all the commandments, which is the most important?" He answered, "Love the Lord your God with all your heart and with all your soul and with *all your mind* and with all your strength" (emphasis mine). Have you ever really thought about what loving God with all your mind means? It is as important as loving God with all your heart.

Everything you've Got

Love springs from trust. Therefore, loving God with all my mind begins with *trusting* God with all my mind. It means asking God to come into the secret places where I may be harboring or practicing sin. It means trusting that He's not going to reject me or forsake me or be totally disgusted with me. *He already knows.* And He wants *in*. He will not clean it out with a big yard blower from the outside. He cleans up the mind from the inside only.

I have had many discussions with other believers over this subject. I can speak to it with some limited degree of insight because I have personally experienced both realities in the course of my life: a tormented mind filled with all sorts of secret junk and a clean mind filled with far more that is wholesome. *Old Man Junk* still likes to walk down the corridors of my mind as often as he can, but God has taught me and continues to enable me not to invite him to sit down and make himself at home.

The reason I remain adamant about the potential every person has to be free *through and through* is not only because the Word of God says they can, but because I cannot imagine a harder core case than I was. If God can change, free, and cleanse *my* mind after all the horrid pictures that were papered on the walls, He can change, free, and cleanse *anyone's*.

But, we have to cooperate. How do we do that? We apply the principle of feeding what we want to live and starving what we want to die. In other words, we start feeding the Spirit in us and starving the flesh.

In many of the discussions I've had with other believers, numbers still claim what I used to claim: "But I don't feed the flesh." Meanwhile, they, like I used to do, still watch some inappropriate programming, "occasional" R-rated movies but "not the really bad kind," and engage in impure or unedifying conversation and humor.

Much too often we have adopted a relative standard based on the wickedness of the world rather than the holiness of God. Because we don't do and watch most of the "stuff out there," our minds are clean. Yet in reality, they are not. One of the seductive lies of Satan is to name things *harmless* that are anything but.

Here's the deal. We don't know how harmful and effective all these "lesser evils than the really depraved world" are until we've given them up for awhile. We think our minds are clean. Until they really *are* clean. Can we keep them spotless? No. Clean? Yes!

Please hear me out. We are living in radical times. We have waltzed into a season on the Kingdom calendar that is unprecedented. We have entered the age of escalation: escalating evil, escalating deception, escalating seduction, and thankfully an escalating outpouring of the Holy Spirit. God has not left us ill-equipped to stand victoriously while surrounded by ever increasing wickedness.

We are living in a time of unparalleled release of the Word of God upon the lives of laypeople. Never before has the entire globe experienced such a wave of scriptural equipping. Laypeople all over the world are testifying to a growing hunger for the Word of God. What is God doing? He is arming His people with the sword of the Spirit because we've entered an unprecedented war!

Not coincidentally, God has also equipped us with more uncompromising media and materials than any generation before us have ever had, suited for everything from Christian growth to Christian entertainment. In the United States, we have access to innumerable Christian tapes and CDs. We have all sorts of Christian magazines of excellent quality. We have tremendously well-written Christian novels. We have more Christian programming than ever before. In comparison to secular programming, it may not be much, but it is a far cry from previous generations that didn't have nearly the need. God has not left us ill-equipped, but we have to take Him up on the equipment!

At first the transition is difficult. We have been so over-stimulated in the world that we've become desensitized to anything less than "much." When we first make the choice to really allow God to sanctify our minds and we start feeding our spirits rather than our flesh, we can "feel" the sacrifice. If we'll keep it up, however, soon we'll start reaping some of the benefit.

Romans 8:6 says, "The mind controlled by the Spirit is life and peace." It's *fabulous!* As we begin to get a taste of this effervescent life and genuine mental peace, we have just the motivation we need to keep up the good work. Then our feelings start changing and improving. We often feel better all over. We start feeling "full" and satisfied. After awhile, it's the only life for us, and we don't ever want to go back.

Yes, the kind of transition I'm describing is radical, but we're living in radical times. The lion wants in the yard, and we'd better have a plan to keep him out. Peter learned the hard way how much access the devil wants to devour believers. He had gotten in Peter's yard. The apostle's advice to us? "Prepare your minds for action; be self-controlled; . . . As obedient children, do not conform to the evil desires you had when you lived in ignorance" (1 Pet. 1:13–14).

If you haven't already surrendered to the pursuit of loving God with your whole mind and trusting Him to sanctify your thoughts, why not start now? You will be freer and more contented than you've ever been in your life! Not only that, you have no idea what disaster could befall you if you don't let God clean up what's behind the hole in the wall. Why not let Him shine His light on it and clean it up?

Then through the empowering of His Holy Spirit, start furnishing the mind with "whatever is true, whatever is noble, whatever is right, whatever is pure, whatever is lovely, whatever is admirable—anything (that) is excellent or praiseworthy" (Phil. 4:8). You might be surprised to discover how many things can fall into those categories—like a great play, a night at the symphony, a good book, or a fabulous basketball game. God wants to be in our leisure time as much as He is in our church and our work.

Beloved, sometimes nothing is more spiritual than recreative refreshment! Don't withhold it from Him. Remember, the protective kind of sanctification comes when He is invited into our *through and through.*

What's out there in the world's entertainment media is only going to get worse. At what point are we going to opt out of its direct influence? We've got a job to do out there in that dark world. Those people out there are our assignment. How can we minister to them if we're altogether like them? What else but God's lavish presence in our lives will distinguish us from *all the other people on the face of the earth*? (Exod. 33:16).

Oh, beloved. Let's do this thing . . . and let's do it to the core. Fortified lives: from the walls around our courtyards to the secret, inner courts of the mind. What have you got to lose that's not worth the loss? And just wait until you experience the gain! We are standing at a crossroad and, as the writer of Proverbs says, wisdom is crying out. "Beside the gates leading to the city, at the entrances, she cries aloud" (Prov. 8:3). I have an idea that at this point we all know some things wisdom is telling us to do. Let's do them. — Jackie, Dang it!

PART III

THE WAY
HOME

CHAPTER 12

NAME CALLING

My name is *Had*. You may know me, but you may not know my new name. You may have no idea what I've been through because I do my best to look the same. I am scared to death of you. I used to be just like you. I once held my head up high without propping it on my hymnal.

I was well respected back then, and I even respected myself. I was wholeheartedly devoted to God, and if the truth be known, somewhere deep inside I was sometimes the slightest bit proud of my devotion. Then I'd repent . . . because I knew that was wrong. I didn't want to be wrong. Not ever.

People looked up to me. And life looked good from up there. I felt good about who I was. That was before I was *Had*. Strangely, I no longer remember my old name. I just remember I liked it. I liked who I was. I wish I could go back. I wish I'd just wake up. But I fear I'm wide awake. I have had a nightmare. And the nightmare was me. *Had*.

If I could really talk to you and you could really listen, I'd tell you I have no idea how all this happened. Honestly, I was just like you. I didn't plan to be *Had*. I didn't want to be *Had*. One day I hadn't, then the next day I had.

Oh, I know now where I went wrong. I have rewound the nightmare a thousand times, stopping it right at the point where I departed the trail of good sense. The way ahead didn't look wrong. It just looked different. Strange, he didn't look like the devil in the original scene. But every time I replayed it, he dropped another piece of his masquerade. When he finally took off his mask, he was laughing at me. Nothing seems funny anymore. I will never laugh again as long as he is laughing.

If only I could go back. I would see it this time! I would walk around the trap camouflaged by the brush, and I would not be *Had*. I would be *Proud*. Was that my old name? *Proud*? I can't even remember who I was anymore. I thought I was *Good*. Not *Proud*. But I don't know anymore.

Would you believe I never heard the trap shut? Too many voices were shouting in my head. I just knew I got stuck somewhere unfamiliar, and soon I didn't like the scenery anymore. I wanted to go home. My ankle didn't even hurt at first. Not until the infection set in. Then I thought I would die.

I lay like a whimpering doe while the wolf howled in the darkness. I got scared. I pulled the brush over me and hid. Then I felt like I couldn't breathe. I had to get out of there or I was sure it would kill me. I didn't belong there. I refused to die there.

I pulled and pulled at the trap, but the foothold wouldn't budge. The blood gushed. I had no way out. I screamed for God. I told Him where I was and the shape I was in. He came for me.

The infection is gone. He put something on it and cleaned it up instantly. As He inspected my shattered ankle, I kept waiting for Him to say, "You deserved this, you know. You've been *Had*." Because I did and I know and I have. He hasn't said it yet. I don't know whether He will or not. I don't know how much to trust Him yet. I've never known Him from this side. My leg still hurts. God says it will heal with time. But I fear I will always walk with a limp.

You see, I wrestled with the devil and he gave me a new name. *Had*.

All sorts of people may read this chapter. People who want to help *Had*. People who want to judge *Had*. People who want to know how bad was *Had*. And people who want to know how sorry is *Had*. They can read it if they want, but this part is not for them. It's just for you. *Had*.

In case no one has said it to you yet, I sure am sorry you've been *Had*. It's horrible, isn't it? Devastating not to live up to your own expectation. To become such a pauper to *Grace*. I've been *Had* a time or two myself. It's been awhile, but I remember well what it was like being him.

God says He doesn't want me to forget. I asked Him why. He said too many people have been *Had* out there. All sorts of ways to be *Had*. *Good* and *Proud* think there are just a few, but if they're not careful, they may be *Wrong*. And someday they may even be *Had*. But I don't hope so. I don't wish anyone to be *Had*. I used to wish I could be *Good* and *Proud* again, but I don't anymore. I don't want to be *Good, Proud,* or *Had*. I just want to be *Healed*.

God says He will never let me be so *Healed* that I forget about *Had*. There have been more *Hads* than *Good* and *Proud* may ever know. Sometimes it takes a *Has Been* to know a *Had*.

One thing is for sure. *Had* needs a lot of *Help*. *Healed's* nickname is *Help*. He got the name because he is what he does. He can't stop. *Healed Hads Help*.

God wanted to make sure I never act like I haven't been *Had*. So He left the scars. He kept a set on His own hands and feet and left one on my ankle. That's OK. My scars bear the marks of death. Don't let anyone tell you that being *Had* won't kill you. It will. It was meant to. If it doesn't, you've been *Had* for nothing and you'll be *Had* again.

Christ raises the dead only after they die. Before I was *Had*, God kept saying, "You are not yet *Dead*." So instead I was *Had*. Christ let Lazarus lie dead for four days, but not because He was mean. Scripture says He loved Lazarus even though He let the illness kill him.

Perhaps we all need to know how it feels to be dead for awhile. But do we believe we might see the glory of God? That's what Christ told Martha she would see. When He raised Lazarus from the dead, Christ did not raise Him sick. He raised him *Healed*. I have a suspicion that Lazarus never got to kid himself into thinking he couldn't get sick again. He just asked for *Grace* never to be *Had* again.

Come on, *Had*. Let's you and I go on a walk together. It's time for you to go home. Maybe to a part of God's home where you've never even been. I'll walk you part of the way, and we'll talk. You don't have to hang your head with me. Then again, you can if you want. You can cry, get mad, throw rocks, and kick at the dirt.

Been there. Just keep walking.

CHAPTER 13

STARTING HOME

All you need to get started is to know you need to get started. Very likely you are somewhere between having a thousand feelings and having none at all. That's OK.

Can you think with your head rather than your heart? Can you think with that one little part of your mind that God kept covered with His hand, protected from corruption and confusion?

The truth is still in there, and He's telling you what to do. Follow what you know to be true. Do what His Word says. Disregard some of the ways you feel right now.

Your heart has been so misshapen by the twists of Satan's lies that you'd better not trust it for a while. You'll know when your heart is starting to get well. It will hurt so badly with throbbing pangs of repentance, you'll think you're going to die. And you will. Then God will raise you from the very thing that has been the death of you. He really will give you a future.

I ask you, in fact I would beg you if that would make a difference, to do several things at this point of the journey. Remember that seductions can come in all sorts of forms. In case your seduction is one Satan used to tempt you to leave your family or to divorce your spouse, if it's not too late, don't! You are not in any shape to make those kinds of decisions, and the destroyer must destroy no more. Don't let Satan have another inch. The first piece of armor you've got to put back on is the breastplate of righteousness. Your injured heart will be protected by your *doing* what is right until you *feel* what is right.

Satan wants you to feel hopeless. He is a liar. You belong to God. Tighten that helmet of salvation around your head. Know that you know you are His and nothing has ripped you from His hand. If need be, take a pen and write in the margin several times: "I am God's."

You may wish you could flee from God's presence, . . . but if you rise on the wings of the dawn and if you settle on the far side of the sea, even there His hand will guide you, and His right hand will hold you fast (Ps. 139:9–10). He made a blood covenant with you, and He is faithful when we are faithless.

Somewhere along the way, the enemy talked you into lowering your shield of faith, and you were no longer able to extinguish his fiery darts. Perhaps he came at you with the same words he used to seduce Eve: "Did God really say . . . ?" Yes, He really said. Your shield is right where you left it. Pick it back up and choose to believe He is who He says He is, and He'll do what He says He'll do. We can't humanize God even when we, mortal men, have turned out to be so different from whom we said we were.

Because you know it's your only ticket to freedom, by a sheer act of your will, chain yourself to the wrist of Christ and start taking your first steps out of the darkness. You probably don't trust anyone right now, and you're not even sure you can trust God. You can. But you'll learn all that for yourself. No one can really tell you what you're about to learn for yourself—if you're willing.

Don't worry about the future right now. Just offer Him your wrist and tell Him to drag you home even if you're not sure you belong or even want to go. You do. You're just too wounded right now to feel it. "As for you, because of the blood of my covenant with you, I will free your prisoners from the waterless pit. Return to your fortress, O prisoners of hope" (Zech. 9:11–12).

I want to ask you to do another critical thing if you haven't already come to this step. Muster up every bit of the courage you have within you and ask God to baptize you in a tide of sorrow over your sin. Ask Him to do it for as long as necessary until full repentance comes.

I beg you not to be afraid of this kind of sorrow. The Bible calls this "godly sorrow," and it is the most wonderful thing that can happen to you in the next little while. You cannot be restored until it comes.

Don't misunderstand me. I don't want you waiting on this sorrow to come before you walk away from your darkness. We've already established that the decision to go home is often an act of volition based on what you know to be true. Often you have to walk away from the seductive clutches of the evil one to begin feeling the health of godly sorrow.

Ask Christ to come get you. Tell Him that you are willing to leave. Then ask the Holy Spirit who has been temporarily quenched to come and do His job. Be patient until He does. The tide may come in rather slowly, but if you belong to God, it will come. It must. Godly sorrow will lead to repentance (2 Cor. 7:10).

For those who have been *wholehearted, sincerely, and purely devoted to Christ* but found themselves seduced by the serpent into some realm of ungodliness, genuine repentance cannot help but come. There are counterfeits to be sure, but the difference is in the fruit.

Tragically, inauthentic repentance is exactly what has given Christian restoration a bad name. If we're still able to strut around like an arrogant rooster, something's wrong. That's not repentance. But when true repentance comes (feeling more like a dead duck), God will not hesitate for a moment to forgive, cast the sins in the sea of forgetfulness, and put the child on the road to restoration.

Who are we as the Body of Christ, likewise weak in our natural selves, to be a harsher judge than the one-and-only righteous God? We must be thinking with our own deceptive hearts because we certainly are not thinking with our Head.

Our Head, Jesus Christ, said, "Why are you thinking these things in your hearts? Which is easier: to say, 'Your sins are forgiven,' or to say, 'Get up and walk'? But that you may know that the Son of Man has authority on earth to forgive sins. . . ." He said to the paralyzed man, "I tell you, get up, take your mat and go home" (Luke 5:22–24).

Do you care about a fellow believer, *Had,* who is feeling a bit paralyzed? Why don't you and I remove a few tiles on the nearest roof and place him "right in front of Jesus"?

James 2:12–13 says:

> So speak and act as [people should] who are
> to be judged under the law of liberty [the moral

instruction given by Christ, especially about love].

For to him who has shown no mercy the judgment [will be] merciless; but mercy [full of glad confidence] exults victoriously over judgment. (AMP)

The NIV says mercy triumphs over judgment, but I just can't help myself. I'd rather exult! Why don't we exult to give mercy? God does.

> Who is a God like you,
>> who pardons sin and forgives the transgression
>> of the remnant of his inheritance?
> You do not stay angry forever
>> but delight to show mercy.
> You will again have compassion on us;
>> you will tread our sins underfoot
>> and hurl all our iniquities into the depths of
>> the sea. (Micah 7:18–19)

Fear. I think that's why. We in our injured flesh are so scared someone will make a fool out of us. Ah, but I'd rather mercy make a fool of me than judgment. I will choose to believe the repentant.

Does God not look upon the heart? Does He not know what to do with insincerity? Is He not after all the One against whom any offense of inauthenticity comes? Will He not chastise His own? And even then will His firm discipline not be to chase the insincerity back into the abyss, so that He can delight to give mercy?

If the Bible is about anything at all, it is about God having mercy on the pitiful plight of men, forgiving their sins and restoring their lives. Christ never resisted the truly repentant, but the Pharisees on the other hand could really get to Him.

Had, you don't want to be like the Pharisees. Better to admit where you're not and ask God's help to get you where you need to be. Do not fake a manifestation of the Spirit that isn't there. Have no confidence in your flesh. Just be real before Him. That's what He wants from you. That's what He wants from all of us.

To some who were confident of their own righteousness and looked down on everybody else, Jesus told this parable:

> Two men went up to the temple to pray, one a
> Pharisee and the other a tax collector. The Pharisee
> stood up and prayed about himself: "God, I thank
> you that I am not like other men—robbers, evil-
> doers, adulterers—or even like this tax collector. I
> fast twice a week and give a tenth of all I get."
>
> But the tax collector stood at a distance. He
> would not even look up to heaven, but beat his
> breast and said, "God, have mercy on me, a
> sinner."
>
> I tell you that this man, rather than the other,
> went home justified before God. For everyone
> who exalts himself will be humbled, and he who
> humbles himself will be exalted. (Luke 18:10–14)

Dear *Had,* that's what Christ is looking for as you find your way back. The way home is humility. Make no excuses. Rationalize nothing. Blame no one. Humble yourself. If you don't yet feel the sorrow that you know will be necessary, ask Him for it like a beggar asks for bread.

Humble yourself, dear one. Come in total weakness to Him. "Grieve, mourn and wail. Change your laughter to mourning and your joy to gloom. Humble yourselves before the Lord, and he will lift you up" (James 4:9–10). And one day He will faithfully turn your mourning into dancing.

> In those days John the Baptist came, preaching
> in the Desert of Judea and saying, "Repent, for the
> kingdom of heaven is near." . . . People went out
> to him from Jerusalem and all Judea and the
> whole region of the Jordan. Confessing their sins,
> they were baptized by him in the Jordan River.
>
> But when he saw many of the Pharisees and
> Sadducees coming to where he was baptizing, he
> said to them: "You brood of vipers! Who warned
> you to flee from the coming wrath? Produce fruit
> in keeping with repentance." (Matt. 3:1–2, 5–8)

True repentance bears fruit. I am utterly convinced that a man or woman who has been *wholehearted, sincerely, and purely devoted to Christ* and who has gone through the horror of seduction will come out of it with a humility that can last a lifetime. You see, God forgives and forgets because He does not need to remember. We are forgiven but do not forget because we are wise never to lose sight of where we've been and how God has rescued us.

True repentance also bears the fruit of gratitude. Have you ever just wept before the Lord when all you could whisper was, "Thank You, God. Oh, thank You, God"? *Healed Hads* do it all the time. You're going to be one of those one day—if you're not already. All in due time.

I don't recommend this particular process and have to believe there's got to be a better way, but there's nothing quite like a fresh brush with the lifesaving mercy of God to jump-start your stale spiritual senses. Our human natures think so little of God, even in our huge religiosity, until we are forced to think more. Ironically, we need to come to the place where we're desperate enough to consider, "If God's not bigger than I have thus far needed and believed Him to be, I am history."

I shared with you that I wrote this book while in a tiny cabin looking out a picture window at my favorite stretch of mountains. My intention was to hardly lay eyes on a mortal, but when Keith came for a few days, he found me a tad under the weather. He claimed he was taking me for a drive and drove me straight to a doctor.

The physician in the clinic was a woman just about my age. As she listened to my heart, I listened to hers. It was quiet and cold, but it said a lot. "Do you wake up every day of your life in a total state of disbelief and gratitude for the beauty you behold around here?" She looked up at me like I was crazy. Of course, it may not have been my question that startled her. It may have been the dog tag I was wearing around my neck right by her stethoscope that said, "Holy to the Lord" in big black letters. It had come in an envelope with a Bible study I had been doing back home. I decided I'd just wear it while I was writing for the extra reminder of sanctification.

I wanted to say, "I really am normal," but I knew she would know I was lying. After all, she was listening to my heart.

She finally answered my question. "Well. Not so much anymore. I've lived here a year now."

A year? And you've already lost your wonder? You just got through telling me you were late to work because five moose wouldn't get out of the road. And you're used to this? What in the world is wrong with you? Give me that stethoscope! You're the one that's ill!

That's what I was thinking, but all I said was, "I don't live here, but I've been here many times. I can't imagine ever getting used to the beauty of it all."

She shrugged and wrote me a prescription. She told me she believed in fate. I told her I believed in God. My heart broke for her when I left, and I prayed for God to write her a prescription. Jesus. Just one dose. That's all she needed.

My doctor didn't need a thing I, too, hadn't needed in my disappointment with life. Not only did she imply she had never been *Found;* she gave me the coldest impression that she had never escaped from the devil long enough to find herself *Had.* "The god of this age has blinded the minds of unbelievers, so that they cannot see the light of the gospel of the glory of Christ, who is the image of God" (2 Cor. 4:4). May the irresistible convicting power of the Holy Spirit unveil her eyes! True repentance sees the beauty, and *Healed Hads* don't get over it.

True repentance also swells grace. Reflect for a moment on our previous chapter. At first *Had* is humiliated to become such a pauper to Grace but when all is said and done, Grace healed *Had*. Now he knows what Peter, the *Sifted*, meant by the words "But grow in the grace and the knowledge of our Lord and Savior Jesus Christ" (2 Pet. 3:18).

We grow in many ways, but too few believers, if not offered a little extra incentive, grow in grace. Nothing is natural about growing in grace. Oh, that we would willingly! But if not willingly, oh, that we would not fail in opportunity!

Had, here's the deal. You will never be able to go back to *Have Not*. *Proud* is totally out of the question, and "No one is *good*— except God alone" (Luke 18:19, emphasis mine). But you can go forward with what *Hads* can have. You can have an extra dose of humility. You can have a fresh wave of gratitude. And you can have a growth spurt of *Grace*. So can every other believer, but somehow *Hads* can be a little more likely to have. It's up to you.

CHAPTER 14

A PATH OF HOPE
AND RESTORATION

God wrote this section of the book on my heart after an argument. Not a terribly heated one but an argument nonetheless.

Why the small group of us had the audacity to sit around and discuss a brother's life, especially one we had never met, is a mystery to me. But, as our natures would have it, that's what we did. A Christian singer who had ministered to tens of thousands had tumbled headlong into a fall. I only know that because he said it of himself. Otherwise, I, like my grandmother, would have thought "folks oughter be mindin' their own bidnis."

This singer had admitted his sin, and as if the pain they all were suffering was not enough, the Christian world began casting their votes as to whether or not he should ever "be allowed" to sing Christian music again. I do declare, I think I'm about to get angry again just thinking about it. As I live and breathe, I cannot find a single time in Scripture when God called upon the popular vote of man to help Him deliver a verdict over one of His children.

217

Goodness knows most of the population would be condemned to the fiery reaches by now.

God does not look on the outward appearance of things. He makes His decisions based upon what He sees in the heart (1 Sam. 16:7). He may set some people aside for no apparent reason, leaving the Body baffled. Others He uses more mightily than ever after something we think is utterly terminal, and the Body is horrified. Why? *God knows things we don't know. He looks upon the heart.* And, by the way, He doesn't take very kindly to people telling Him how to do His job.

I went to bed that night very disturbed. I tossed and turned as I thought about my own tumultuous young life and how much grace and patience God had shown me as He taught—and was *still* teaching—this Mephibosheth how to walk on legs that had been handicapped for so long. I wondered, *Have I come just a half a cup short of all the grace I'm going to get? Is there a limited supply?* If so, I felt rather like David in Psalm 101:2 when he confidently announced to God, "I will be careful to lead a blameless life"! Then, as if he considered about how long he thought he could keep it up, he followed his vow with the words, "When will you come to me?"

I think maybe David thought he could keep it up until sundown if God wouldn't mind coming to get him before dinner. I know the feeling! I also thought of countless others who were like me and had required a generous helping of second chances to learn how to keep their wagons between the ditches. None of us had been so "blessed" with a public trial as our popular brother.

I brought all sorts of questions before the Lord. "Am I that off base? Am I just softhearted because I have been such a grace project myself? Have I lost my balance? Did I ever have any? I know he needs help and could really use a break, but is he a castaway in evangelical America? Or can he stay but better never open his mouth to sing again?" I finally drifted off to sleep, praying for him.

The next morning, I picked up where I had left off the day before in the novice Bible study I was writing for my class in Houston. This study would later become the series *A Heart like His* on the life of David. My previous day's research had ended with Saul's confirmation as king at the end of 1 Samuel 11. As only God would have it, my text for that day's study was Samuel's instruction to the people of Israel after their admission of grievous sin. God answered my question as boldly and quickly as He has ever answered me, and goodness knows, I've asked Him plenty.

Before I share with you what He revealed to me from Scripture, I want you to hear my heart. The last thing I'm suggesting is that I have some definitive answer to restoration or that my outlook is the right outlook. I am a fellow traveler just like you, simply trying to wade my way through Scripture for a few answers to some tough questions. We were not all meant to think exactly alike. The Body of Christ is made up of many parts and variegated giftings.

I understand that there must be those who take the hard line and make it tough for people to come back again so they will not take the grace of God lightly. I do believe people in the spotlight have a major responsibility regarding the Body of Christ. I also believe in discipline and have certainly been on the other end of God's chastising rod more than a few times. And most assuredly

I believe in *repentance,* the *real* kind. The *radical* kind. Still, this side of the fence is where I belong. I would be nothing less than a hypocrite if I refused a brother and sister the right to draw from the bottomless well of God's grace and try again. I had to learn to swim in it to live.

This section has been written on my heart for ten years but has never made its way to paper. I believe now that it was waiting for the rest of this book to grow around it. I am usually very conscious of a concept for a book growing. Oddly, the concept for this book came complete, God delivering the title to me *in full.* My Bible was open to these verses for the first time in a long while, and the instruction from the Lord came so unmistakably that I dated it in the margin: *April 19, 2000.* My pen still didn't touch the paper until almost exactly a year later when I knew His Spirit was saying to me, "Now." I headed to the mountains, and within a few weeks it was done.

I was much too young, much too inexperienced, and needed the approval of others much too much to write something like this a decade ago. And, incidentally, no one was asking me. I had far more zeal at that time than knowledge, and God wasn't letting me out much. The beauty of it was, I didn't even know it. I'm not sure why He lets me out now. My teachers have already forgotten more than I'll ever know, and I still maintain that in my natural personality, I am blonder than I pay to be. I still pay big bucks to be blonde, but I've learned a few things with every one of those gray hairs I'm covering.

Over the last ten years, I have had the opportunity to thumb through these very passages with many a sister and even a few brothers whose knees were pretty bloody from some kind of tumble. Not too long ago, God quarantined a minister of the gospel and me toward the back of a plane right across from one another. I did not know him personally, but I could tell his soul was deeply troubled. Later he told me he had made a decision of some kind that he deeply regretted. We studied these Scriptures together all the way to our destination. I was so humbled to be able to serve him.

First Samuel 12:20–25 represents some of the clearest ABC concepts for restoration that I've ever found in a single location of Scripture. We will give them much attention over the next several chapters. I will not do them justice, but may God take them and walk you through them with Spirit-filled comprehension. May they become a path of clarity and hope to you. I want you to know that I'm honored to serve you, *Had*. If you'll take off your shoes, I'll gladly get on my knees and wash your feet in the water of this Word.

In response to the people of Israel's admission of grievous sin against God, Samuel, God's chosen prophet or spokesman to them, responded with the following words found in 1 Samuel 12:20–25:

> "Do not be afraid," Samuel replied. "You have done all this evil; yet do not turn away from the LORD, but serve the LORD with all your heart. Do not turn away after useless idols. They can do you no good, nor can they rescue you, because they are useless. For the sake of his great name the LORD will not reject his people, because the LORD was pleased to make you his own. As for

me, far be it from me that I should sin against the
LORD by failing to pray for you. And I will teach
you the way that is good and right. But be sure to
fear the LORD and serve him faithfully with all
your heart; consider what great things he has done
for you. Yet if you persist in doing evil, both you
and your king will be swept away."

Through the next several chapters, we will take each precept
individually, considering how it applies to a New Testament believer.
We don't have to make any big reaches for application. Israel's situation was conceptually identical to someone being seduced from his
or her *wholehearted, sincere, and pure devotion* to God for lesser—
even *spiritual* or *earthly acceptable*—things. God's people are not to
be like the world and take on the habits of surrounding pagans, nor
are we ever to allow something that even seems spiritual or reasonable to disconnect us from the Head (Col. 2:19).

Added to all of Israel's other sins against God, they had committed the evil of asking for an earthly, visible king (1 Sam.
12:19). I wonder what all the ways might be that we perhaps even
unknowingly pivot our primary devotions to the visible princes
of the earth, whether animate or inanimate?

God had always had in mind to raise up a royal line among
His people through which He would eventually present His Son,
the Messiah, and the King of all kings. The heinous nature of
Israel's sin against God was their attitude and motive. God had
delivered them from the hands of their enemies on every side and
caused them to live securely (1 Sam. 12:11), but Samuel narrated
what happened next:

"But when you saw that Nahash king of the
Ammonites was moving against you, you said to
me, 'No, we want a king to rule over us'—even
though the LORD your God was your king. Now
here is the king you have chosen, the one you
asked for; see, the LORD has set a king over you.
(1 Sam. 12:12–13)

Piercing words had already come from the prophet Samuel
from the moment Saul was appointed king:

Samuel summoned the people of Israel to the
LORD at Mizpah and said to them, "This is what
the LORD, the God of Israel, says: 'I brought Israel
up out of Egypt, and I delivered you from the
power of Egypt and all the kingdoms that
oppressed you. But you have now rejected your
God, who saves you out of all your calamities and
distresses. And you have said, 'No, set a king over
us.'" (1 Sam. 10:17–19)

Have you noticed that big trouble can begin when we start
saying no to something God has provided for us and look for our
own more rational and reasonable means of provision? Food for
thought. Mind you, this king who became a misleading idol to
them, stealing their devotion, had the Spirit of God upon him. It
doesn't always happen like that, but don't forget that it *can.*

Thankfully, our God of inconceivable grace and patience
did not leave them *nor us* without remedy. The very fact that He

assigned it to the annals of inspired Scripture means it has something to say to us. With this foundation poured, in the next chapter we'll begin going through each precept of the prescription God wrote His children on the tongue of the prophet Samuel.

CHAPTER 15

TREKKING WITH FACTS, NOT FEAR

In this chapter we're going to examine each phrase of 1 Samuel 12:20–25. This passage provides us a road map for restoration.

"DO NOT BE AFRAID" (V. 20)

When we've really been *Had* and we're beginning to wake up to what is happening, one of the first, most inundating waves of emotion is fear. I find it interesting and infuriating that Satan subtly talks people into things then proceeds to taunt and terrorize them with fear.

Later in the prescription God wrote through the prophet Samuel we'll see the appropriate kind of fear. All others come from Satan and our flesh nature.

The enemy can fuel fear in a *Had* through three primary areas: (1) fear of consequences, (2) fear of men, and (3) fear of future circumstances. *Had*, you probably have never been in a position where you have been so forced to trust in the sovereignty of God.

You will either learn to trust Him as never before, or you will be impaired for the rest of your life. Choose trust and live. Your God is in the heavens and He is all wise. He will not appoint any chastisement nor allow any consequences that cannot be used *for* you when all is said and done.

I want you to enlist the support of several people of godly integrity who know how to war in prayer. Together start binding the enemy from any further work where your situation is concerned. Pray according to Matthew 16:19, asking God to bind Satan and to loose the Holy Spirit upon every single detail. Bind it from Satan in Jesus' powerful name, and loose it to the full, trustworthy work of God through His Holy Spirit.

As you and several others agree (Matt. 18:19–20) in binding the enemy, whatever is loosed, even if it is temporarily painful, will be from heaven and not from hell and will work for your good. Every day for the duration of your healing process you are going to need to concentrate on Scriptures that speak of trusting God. Completely humble and surrender yourself and all things concerning you into His loving hands and His wise plan.

> For though the Lord is high, yet has He
> respect to the lowly [bringing them into fellowship
> with Him]; but the proud and haughty He knows
> and recognizes [only] at a distance. Though I walk
> in the midst of trouble, You will revive me; You
> will stretch forth Your hand against the wrath of
> my enemies, and Your right hand will save me.
> The Lord will perfect that which concerns me;
> Your mercy and loving-kindness, O Lord, endure

for ever; forsake not the works of Your own hands.
(Ps. 138:6–8 AMP)

Ask God to empower you not to let your heart melt over the fear of men. David wrote:

> When I am afraid
> I will trust in you.
> In God, whose word I praise,
> in God I trust; I will not be afraid.
> What can mortal man do to me?" (Ps. 56:3–4)

Christ said to His disciples in matters of much more frightening consequences than yours, "Do not be afraid of those who kill the body but cannot kill the soul. Rather, be afraid of the One who can destroy both soul and body in hell" (Matt. 10:28). Proverbs 29:25 wisely points out that fear of man will prove to be a snare.

In more public situations, you may be tempted to worry about what people are saying. You're going to have to release them and your pride entirely to the Lord. You'll even have to let go of your overwhelming desire at times to take up for yourself as gossipers may talk about things they don't even know.

Your responsibility is getting entirely back on track with God. Your pride is going to take a beating through this whole thing, but keep in mind that the sifting of our proud natures is one of God's primary divine intentions. God wants all our pride not only to take a beating but a killing! Those who haven't been *Had* by seduction but are *Had* by pride are in terrible trouble in their own right. God has no use for pride. It's one of the few things

Scripture points out that He absolutely hates. Every time God steps on your pride through all of this and it yells, "Ouch!" ask Him to go ahead and stomp on it until He kills the wicked thing.

I realize it hurts when others talk. Especially those you truly care about so much. Trust God to use time to tell of your restored and even previously exceeded godly character as He sifts the tares from the wheat of your life. "For it is God's will that by doing good you should silence the ignorant talk of foolish men" (1 Pet. 2:15).

Seek God's approval with everything in you, and ask for the empowering of His Spirit not to let your sin make you a servant of men. If you're a pastor or church staff member, I don't mean that you may not have to submit yourself to a disciplinary season by those in authority over you. Bowing to the biblically imposed chain of authority is critically important and may be a vital part of the process God wants to use to restore you. Still, you must be careful not to slip into the trap of seeking human approval over God's. "Am I now trying to win the approval of men, or of God? Or am I trying to please men? If I were still trying to please men, I would not be a servant of Christ" (Gal. 1:10).

During seasons of fear in my own life, I have soaked myself in the balm of Psalm 27. Dear one, consider doing the same. You're going to have to believe and count on God's Word as you never have before to come out of your season as a *Healed Had*.

"YOU HAVE DONE ALL THIS EVIL" (V. 20)

As hard as this part of the process is to handle, it is one of the most critical. If you shirk it in any way, you will never be free. Do not in any way downplay the seriousness of any sin you have committed before God or before those who must know for you to get the help you need. Do not give in to the temptation to transfer your sin, blame it, or rationalize it. Do not dream of minimizing it in comparison to what you may reason are "bigger sins."

For instance, if you are a married man or woman who became very emotionally attached to someone besides your spouse, do not even think of minimizing your betrayal by reasoning that nothing physical happened. Take full responsibility before God for the betrayal of your heart. Take responsibility before your spouse if she or he already suspects such a thing and will not be further devastated by the confession. Confess it to anyone else who is absolutely necessary in your full restorative process.

In matters concerning pastors and ministers, I cannot imagine their church families being edified by details or graphics of certain kinds of sins that prey visually upon the mind. Those with far more wisdom than I must counsel you if you are in such a situation. If sins have been committed against a church body or a group of people, forgiveness should be sought through a heartfelt confession of a general nature if the details are unedifying. The truly repentant will not be able to keep from begging forgiveness from anyone or any group of people against which he or she has sinned.

Seek counsel from godly men and/or women in authority to know whether certain kinds of confessions could cause more devastation than good. Each situation can be very different and applying hard-and-fast rules to them in a book of this sort would be unwise.

You may be relieved that your situation is not as "serious" as the ones I just described. Caution! That's exactly the kind of attitude I'm warning you to avoid! Whatever your circumstances, if you have been seduced away from your *wholehearted, sincere, and pure devotion to Christ,* something huge has happened, and sin has been involved. The more seriously you take it, the more freedom God will have to deal with it fully and get your precious life back on track. Trust me. I know about this. Remember, in my own way and in my own kind of circumstances, I've been *Had.* I unfortunately know what I'm talking about here.

Come before God and anyone else who is necessary to your healing process, saying without hesitation or a single disclaimer, "I have done all this evil." The closer you have been to God, the more sensitive you are likely to be to all kinds of offenses. Even if others "don't see the big deal," if you have been close enough to God to know it is a big deal, you are wise to make a very big deal of it with Him and whomever else you must to be fully restored. This kind of confession and willingness to take full responsibility will prove to be life to you and the full catalyst of forgiveness and restoration.

"YET DO NOT TURN AWAY FROM THE LORD" (V. 21)

Whatever way you've been *Had* and no matter what you have done, please, please, please don't even consider turning away from the Lord as an option. Remember, that's exactly what the enemy is after! Do you remember the primary goal of the seducing spirits of latter days? "But the (Holy) Spirit distinctly and expressly declares that in latter times some will turn away from the faith, giving attention to deluding and seducing spirits and doctrines that demons teach" (1 Tim. 4:1 AMP). Whatever you do, do not turn away from the faith! In fact, for our present purposes, I implore you not to turn away from *faith*.

What do you really believe about God? What you are going through right now is sure going to help you answer that question. You may be about to find out that some or much of what you've believed wasn't nearly enough or that it wasn't even accurate. Was your faith in yourself and in your ability to be good, righteous, and always wise? Or was your faith in God, who demonstrates (present tense) His own love for us in this: "While we were still sinners, Christ died for us" (Rom. 5:8)?

Scripture is clear that our righteous acts are nothing but filthy rags before God. If your faith is in your own righteousness, you are in big trouble now. It's time to turn away from all the former things your faith may have been in and trade them in for all the things *the faith* truly concerns. Like the finished work of Calvary. Christ didn't cry from the cross, "It is finished all except for that thing that terrible *Had* is going to do in the year _____. I'll have to come up with a different sacrifice for that. Or, then again, I guess he'll just have to go to hell. This death is not enough for him."

Are you going to turn away from your faith, or are you going to believe what God's Word says? Colossians 2:13–15 says:

> When you were dead in your sins and in the
> uncircumcision of your sinful nature, God made
> you alive with Christ. He forgave us *all* our sins,
> having canceled the written code, with its regula-
> tions, that was against us and that stood opposed

to us; he took it away, nailing it to the cross. And
having disarmed the powers and authorities, he
made a public spectacle of them, triumphing over
them by the cross. (emphasis mine)

Every one of your sins and mine were applied to Christ's cross
in advance. Oh, I know what's coming next! Someone's about to
ask if that applies to sins committed after salvation or just those
before. I do believe the above Scripture says *all*. Furthermore, the
entire Book of 1 John is written about developing a fuller fellowship with Christ, and its audience already believed in Christ unto
salvation. To them and us he wrote:

> If we claim to be without sin, we deceive our-
> selves and the truth is not in us. If we confess our
> sins, he is faithful and just and will forgive us our
> sins and purify us from all unrighteousness. If we
> claim we have not sinned, we make him out to be
> a liar and his word has no place in our lives.
> (1 John 1:8–10)

The Word is clear that the work of the cross is finished. One
hundred percent complete. The means of forgiveness and total
purification for every sin we have or will ever commit and obedi-
ently confess has already been accomplished. Here's where it all
comes down: are we going to have faith in God and His Word or
our ridiculously weak and sin-prone selves? A lump fills my throat
as my soul sings words to an old hymn that have become such a
reality to me:

My hope is built on nothing less
Than Jesus' blood and righteousness;
I dare not trust the sweetest frame,
But wholly lean on Jesus' name.
On Christ, the solid Rock, I stand;
All other ground is sinking sand,
All other ground is sinking sand.[1]

"BUT SERVE THE LORD WITH ALL YOUR HEART" (V. 24)

Here is where I may differ from some of the hard-liners. I want to speak directly not just to *Had* right now but to those who are meant to help *Had* heal. I do not believe in any stretch of the imagination that God wills for the church or the Body of Christ to refuse a fallen or otherwise seduced servant who has been *wholeheartedly, sincerely, and purely devoted to Christ* the right to serve again. You may as well hang them with a rope because you will virtually kill them.

Yes, they need to seek sound spiritual and emotional health, and yes, they need to follow through with steps like the ones we're about to discuss, but the goal must be fully restored servants of Jesus Christ. I will not argue that times exist when the type of service may need to change, but to refuse a true servant, which many of these have been, the right to serve at all is nearly to destroy him. I would rather be him (or myself, a former *Had*) at the judgment than the audacious person who enforces such a death sentence on the repentant (James 2:12–13).

I don't even think those who have never before been whole-heartedly devoted and end up falling in their own rebellion ought to be refused the right to serve after complete repentance and an active pursuit toward spiritual wellness. Their failure may be the very thing God uses to sift them and make true foot-washing servants out of them.

The truly repentant are often so purified and humbled by disaster that they are willing to do anything! If persons who claim repentance are still arrogant and unwilling to take respon-sibility, they are probably missing the fruit of repentance. They are a long way from ready. Don't bail out on them even then! Help them, speak the truth in love, and pray them to true repentance!

If returning *Hads* do have the fruit of repentance, make sure they know the goal and don't wait long to use them so they will not lose heart! Make them washers of the cups used in the obser-vance of the Lord's Supper, for heaven's sake, or give them park-ing lot duty (both of which have honor and dignity), but don't take away their right to serve God. That's not your right. That's not my right. It is God's alone.

In Scripture, if Christians had gone too far ever to serve again, He usually struck them dead and took them home. Just ask Ananias and Sapphira (Acts 5). If the believer is still living and bears fruit of repentance, I do not believe God is finished using their lives to serve Him in some way. Seek the wisdom of God! "Brothers, if someone is caught in a sin, you who are spiritual should restore him gently" (Gal. 6:1). And a little humility wouldn't hurt either, since the Word is clear that spiritual men and women of God can fall too (same Scripture).

Please forgive me if I seem to be hard on those who have done the right thing and never fallen. I love the *Have Nots* just as much as the *Hads*. I'm just asking you not to be *Had* by self-righteousness, pride, or judgment in exchange for not being *Had* by other things that seem more wicked. Please have mercy mixed with a heaping cupful of wisdom on old *Had*. He really needs your help right now.

Had, don't you dare get all puffed up about this. Your job is to stay humble and to serve the Lord with all your heart with no thought to big or small things.

The argument that God used to lead me to the restorative concepts in 1 Samuel 12:20–25 focused to a great extent on the subject matter involved in this point. No Christian in his or her right mind would say a repentant *Had* couldn't be forgiven by God or shouldn't be forgiven by others. The controversy seems to concern what *Had* is allowed to do even after he is *Healed*.

You probably recall the general circumstances I shared about the fallen brother who led to the discussion and low-heat argument. The biggest point of contention was over whether or not he should ever be "allowed" to sing or sell Christian music again. I do mean ever. (As if that were our decision.) Some said, "I think he should just go into secular music now and should forget ever singing in Christian arenas again."

Wait a second. And that would accomplish exactly what?

First Samuel 12:20 says not to turn away from the Lord; instead serve Him with all your heart. Likely, the very issue in some *Hads'* lives who lacked complete devotion might have been that they were not serving with all their hearts. Part of their prescription would be to return to serving God, but this time with all their hearts.

Then 1 Samuel 12:21 explicitly says, "Do not turn away after useless idols. They can do you no good, nor can they rescue you, because they are useless." I can't think of a more pointed example of turning to an idol and literally worshiping it than taking a God-given gift or talent and serving the godless world with it from then on. Not only would it be idolatry; the idolatrous world would render the God-given gift or talent useless!

Not only must *Had* be very careful what he does; you and I better be careful what we help *Had* do. Again, if *Had* has no fruit of repentance, he's not just *Had*—he's still *Being Had*. In that case, he has no business serving in places of influence. But this book is almost entirely concerned with *Repentant Had*.

"FOR THE SAKE OF HIS GREAT NAME, THE LORD WILL NOT REJECT HIS PEOPLE" (V. 22)

Thank goodness! You and I need never fear that God will reject one of His own. His Word promises,

> "Never will I leave you;
> never will I forsake you." (Heb. 13:5)

Did you notice why? For the sake of His great name! You see, the Lord will not reject you no matter what you've done to your "great" name. His faithfulness to you is based on His great name! His great name stands even if we fall! Is His name still great? The Lord will not reject you, child. Get a load of this next one!

"BECAUSE THE LORD WAS PLEASED TO MAKE YOU HIS OWN" (V. 22)

Not only are you protected from rejection for the sake of God's great name; it just so happens that the Lord was pleased to make you His own. You'd be wise to say this Scripture several times out loud until both your head and your heart hear it. If you are tenderhearted and as devastated as I have been several times in my life, some of you *Hads* are going to stop for a little while and bawl. Been there. I just might stop here and bawl with you. You just take your time here, and we'll pick up whenever you're ready.

In case you're wondering if that's just one Scripture taken out of context and fear it may not agree with the whole counsel of God's Word, here are a few more:

> He reached down from on high and took hold of
> me;
> > he drew me out of deep waters.
> He rescued me from my powerful enemy,
> > from my foes, who were too strong for me.
> They confronted me on the day of my disaster,
> > but the LORD was my support.
> He brought me out into a spacious place;
> > he rescued me because he delighted
> > > in me. (Ps. 18:16–19)

Love Lifted Me

Did you hear that? He rescued you because He delighted in you. And He who began a good work will be faithful to complete it (Phil. 1:6).

> In love he predestined us to be adopted as his
> sons through Jesus Christ, in accordance with *his
> pleasure* and will. . . . In him we have redemption
> through his blood, the forgiveness of sins, in
> accordance with the riches of *God's grace that he
> lavished on us* with all wisdom and under-
> standing. . . . In him we were also chosen, having
> been predestined according to the plan of *him
> who works out everything in conformity with the
> purpose of his will.* (Eph. 1:5, 7–8, 11, emphases
> mine)

My intention is certainly not to debate predestination. I simply want to point out that the same Mind who knew in advance
you would become one of His children also knew in advance
you'd fall for a deceptive scheme of the evil one. Still, He says you
were adopted with pleasure.

I'm crazy about my husband for about a thousand reasons.
One of the things that I love so much about him is a polite little
saying that he repeats almost every time someone thanks him for
something. He doesn't just say, "You're welcome." He says, "It was
my pleasure." Too very different things. Oh, beloved *Had,* please
hear this with your whole heart. When you say, "Oh, God, thank
You so much for saving me and making me Your child," according to Scripture He doesn't just say, "You're welcome." Hear Him
say to you, "It was My pleasure."

Many times in the months and years to come as *Had* heals,
you're going to find yourself saying, "Oh, God, thank You, thank
You, thank You for rescuing me and doing what it took to deliver

me from a foe that was too strong for me." And His answer will be, "It was My pleasure. I rescued you because I delight in you."

I just want to shout Hallelujah!

Did you notice, as well, in the Ephesians passage that God lavishes His grace on you with all wisdom and understanding? He's not running low. Don't miss the fact that God will work even this out, dear *Had,* in conformity with the purpose of His will. You haven't done the one thing God can't turn around and use together with everything else in your life for good (Rom. 8:28). Oh, how God has used defeats of all different kinds in my life for good! Some time back I wrote in my Bible, "God, there is one thing I would have hated worse than some of the things I've been in my life: what I would've been without them."

Please don't misunderstand or misapply what I just wrote. I despise some of the places I have been in the course of my life. If I had it to do all over again, I would desperately want to follow God in joyful obedience, never veering from His path. The price of an unhealthy heart and soul and of the foolishness of resulting decisions has been enormous.

The memories I have to deal with from my past can be heartlessly haunting. I am so frantic not to veer from the path for the rest of my days that I have become maniacal about seeking wholeness in Him. I hope to pursue His sanctification through and through with total abandon, no matter what the future holds. Many times in all seriousness I have asked God to take me home before I allow Satan to pull me into another pit.

Still, I recognize I had the capacity to have been full of pride and self-righteousness. I would not have been a good choice for a spotless track record. I don't think I could've handled one with grace. Thankfully, others can. When all is said and done, and we see our holy, powerful, transcendent God face-to-face, I would have hated to have been proud and self-righteous in my earthly life more than anything else I could've been. And that's saying a lot.

We'll continue with the prescriptive precepts of 1 Samuel 12:20–25 in the next chapter.

STEPS WITH
INDELIBLE PRINTS

The next two precepts in the prescription God gave the prophet Samuel for the restoration of His children directly assign some responsibilities to others besides *Had.* Let's give them a look.

"AS FOR ME, FAR BE IT FROM ME THAT I SHOULD SIN AGAINST THE LORD BY FAILING TO PRAY FOR YOU" (V. 23)

I not only believe that the surrounding Body of Christ shirks its duty by failing to pray for the full restoration of her *Hads;* I believe the implication of Scripture is that she sins directly against God.

I am not at all a cynic about the Body of Christ. I am so happy to tell you that many people I know and with whom I attend church are true, humble God-seekers. They actively rise to the occasions of forgiveness, mercy, and restoration. Sadly, however, we know there are also the *other kind:* busybodies who love to have something to talk about. Self-appointed judges who love to have folks to sharpen their skills on. Insecure people who feel better and higher if others prove lesser and lower.

Whether we want to face it or not, we have a responsibility to fulfill in the process of *Had*'s full restoration. Fervent intercessory prayer for sinners to be restored accomplishes several integral things:

1. Prayer keeps the hearts of the intercessors pure and loving toward the sinner seeking restoration.

You've probably noticed that it's hard to feel lots of negativity toward people for whom you actively intercede.

2. Prayer brings the part of the Body interceding into agreement, thereby beefing up the power of prayer tremendously (Matt. 18:19–20).

Had needs lots of prayer! And for lots of things! You don't even have to wonder if you're praying the will of God when you ask for the full restoration of one of His children. That is His indisputable desire.

3. Prayer keeps the mouth open before God on the matter rather than open before others.

We have no business gossiping about members of the Body of Christ. If we would turn the time we spent discussing the other's life into prayer time instead, no telling what would happen to the glory of God. Mind you, God sees right through gossip in the name of a prayer request.

4. Prayer guards hearts and minds and causes God to bring peace out of chaos (Phil. 4:6–7).

Lots of chaos can surround a *Had* situation.

5. The prayers of the saints to bind the enemy can . . . bind the enemy!

And prayer to loose the Spirit can do just that: loose the Spirit! (Matt. 16:19). Prayer can be used of God to completely thwart any further plan of the enemy and take back what he stole.

6. The prayers of the saints can be honored by God to block any further damage or destruction.

For instance to a marriage or marriages, a family or families, or an entire congregation.

7. Prayer causes the blessing of the fully redeemed and restored to be shared and to profit many.

In all the years since I was *Had* and after my journey to healing and a greater biblical understanding, I have had both the huge responsibility and privilege of helping some other *Hads* along their ways. Sometimes I've been in a primary role and other times a secondary role. I've watched high school *Hads* gradually heal, college *Hads* gradually heal, and more than a few adult *Hads* gradually heal.

I have cried bitter tears over several *Hads* who refused to do what was necessary and continued *Being Had.* In retrospect, I can say in all honesty that raising my children is the only thing that has brought me greater joy than watching a *Had* be fully restored. I can hardly keep from crying as I see a *Healed Had* singing her heart out for the Jesus she loves more than anything in all the world. I can't keep a grip when I watch a *Healed Had* knock the whole place out with a powerful testimony of God's amazing grace.

Just recently, I watched a *Healed Had* march down an aisle in a sparkling white wedding dress, daring to believe God. I watched a *Healed Had* return to teaching high school Sunday school with the full anointing of the Holy Spirit after a long absence.

I realize as I'm listing them to you that I have no idea how many *Hads* I have watched heal either from close proximity or a distance. I have profited from every last one of them. I am all the richer because they touched my life and because I got the distinct privilege of praying for them. Maybe that's why I love them so. It's hard not to love a *Had* for whom you've prayed.

The list could go on and on, but the point is clear: believers who have been made aware of the situation will fail their responsibility and even sin against God by not praying for the full redemption and restoration of *Had* and all those concerned. Not only that, they will miss an unspeakable blessing.

Before I go any further, *Had,* let me say something with such love to you. I've talked about a number of *Hads* with whom I had the joy of working. I will also tell you that the numbers and weight of responsibility eventually became too much for me to handle one-on-one. That's an important reason I believe God had me write this book.

You may wish we could get in contact with one another and we could work together one-on-one because you think I'm the only person who would understand and not judge you. Dear *Had,* that is so untrue. I'm not the only one. God has those people for you. God has called me to a ministry of teaching His Word. As strongly as I feel about this subject, God would not honor my changing the direction of my ministry, even to the restoration of beloved *Hads.*

In this book I am sharing with you everything I know, and you can count on the fact that I am praying for you. Don't dare let me become a false savior to you. Nothing would be more absurd. I'm just an old *Had* who came face-to-face with the only One who can heal.

"I WILL TEACH YOU THE WAY THAT IS GOOD AND RIGHT" (V. 23)

Had, you need teaching as badly as you have ever needed it in your life. You are in desperate need of good, solid, godly (not just "Christian" or "spiritual") counsel. You need to know how to proceed from where you are now to where God wants you to go. You need to know the way that is *good and right.* Just like mine and countless others, your own vision, perception, and estimation have failed you. You need the help of wise others so you can improve your sight and awareness.

I cannot overemphasize the next statement: you also need to know how and why you took a wrong way. This process will be an extremely important part of your knowing the way from here.

Obviously, had you known what you were getting yourself into, you wouldn't have gone that way. You see, the very nature of a satanic scheme is that it is secretive and cunning. It is meant to trap the unsuspecting. You, like all the rest of us who have been *Had,* need to get biblically educated and take a good look like never before at where and why you went wrong.

You, like the rest of us, are really going to have to humble yourself and admit that you have volumes left to learn. *Even if you're a pastor.* Something went wrong, and you're going to have to learn what it was and how to keep it from ever happening again. Someone godly, wise, and trustworthy needs to help you locate your weaknesses and vulnerabilities. Then you need help to strengthen them and get fortified.

I really want to be bold enough to say that you cannot get through this process wholly restored on your own. You need members of the Body of Christ, and I don't mind telling you, some of them need you!

This point is where good, godly counseling comes in as well as solid Bible study and a fuller understanding of a through-and-through kind of sanctification. I also would like to offer another bold piece of advice. Some of you may think that I have some kind of nerve and that this is none of my business, but remember, you're the one that brought me in by reading the book! As long as I've got your attention, I want to tell you what I've seen work best. I'll go ahead and say up front; it is radical.

In *Had* situations where I've taken a primary role (always as part of a team), I have insisted on *Had* agreeing to an intense time of *detoxification, deprogramming,* and *reprogramming.* I think they are critical, and I want to explain what each means. All of these fall under the category of learning, as Samuel said, *the way that is good and right.*

Detoxification. Think of your present state this way: in one way or another the same serpent that got his fangs into Eve got his fangs into you. How he did it and what happened as a result differs from *Had* to *Had.* In some way, as 2 Corinthians 11:2–3 says, the serpent has *corrupted* and *seduced* your mind. I want you to think of that corruption like a poison, venom, or a toxin.

In order to detoxify, you must cut yourself off from the source or sources and all other connections to the source. You may really need some stiff accountability to accomplish this detoxification, but it is vital that you do.

For example, if you have been stealing money, you need to get away from the source from which you found freedom to steal it. If you have been seduced into Internet pornography, you must be bold enough to cut yourself off from all access to the Internet at home or at work. I don't care if you have to give up your whole computer for awhile, this step is vital. You may find that you are safest never getting on the Internet again and letting others do any research you may need.

You've got to be serious about restoration. Do whatever you have to do to cut off the flow of venom. If you have been involved in an extramarital affair or an illicit relationship of some kind, I don't care if you "think" you're in love with the person; it is nothing but a scheme of the devil. Cut off *all* forms of contact not only to him or her but to any other connection you have to the person. Oh, please do not be foolish enough to stay in contact. Don't rationalize a friendship! Too many have tried, only to stay deceived on one level or another. Part of your "waking up" process will not happen until all ungodly contact has ceased. Get all the help you need to make this move and keep this commitment. It is a *big* ticket to freedom!

Deprogramming. However he may have accomplished it, somehow Satan did a fine job of programming your mind with lies and a lot of junk that needs dumping. Every satanic stronghold involves believing some kind of lie or lies. Seduction involves somehow believing a very subtle arsenal of them.

I am really going to risk getting labeled a fanatic on this one, but I have seen the process work, and I have seen the process fail. The participant's willingness to cooperate with this objective has proved to make a huge difference. For a while, you would be wise to avoid any kind of media entertainment (movies, television, books, magazines, etc.) that encourages corrupt thinking.

Your mind will be very susceptible and sensitive for awhile. What might not bother the person sitting next to you could send you into a tailspin, even a possible relapse. For instance, if you've been seduced by pornography, an R-rated movie would be extremely detrimental. So could many PG-13 ratings. I am not sure what business any of us have watching sexually explicit movies, but Satan could use it more destructively on a *Had* than anyone.

Since I used the example of an extramarital affair in the previous point, I'll use it again to keep the concepts clear. Can you imagine that sitcoms, soap operas, or all manner of programming that give approval to sex outside of marriage (including adultery) would be good for someone who has already been seduced? For awhile, *Had*'s mind is far too sensitive and susceptible to forms of media that will do little more than fuel the kinds of deceptions that were nearly the death of him.

Please consider deprogramming from all sorts of deceptive forms of media until you are fully restored. Then you can make the decision as to whether such programs even have a place in your life. These days we have all sorts of media available to Christians that don't fuel temptation or compromise godly character. The quality and content of Christian magazines, music, and novels have vastly improved over the last decade or so. I believe this was divinely intended so that in a world of increasing wickedness, we'd have plenty of safe alternatives.

Many production companies are even starting to make high-quality movies and videos. Just one example is World Wide Pictures Home Video, which is associated with the Billy Graham Evangelistic Association. Their movies are fabulous, and they use the talents of many recognizable stars who are people of principle.

Celebrate the fact that we no longer have to compromise quality to keep from compromising character. I beg you to consider carefully what goes into your mind. Consider deprogramming from the world's deceptive forms of media for a good while.

Reprogramming. Not only does a *Had* need to *de*program from as many sources of deception as possible, she needs to *re*program with the truth of God's Word. As quickly as possible, get into a good, in-depth Bible study with a small accountability group—even if you're a pastor. Even if you *write* Bible studies, for heaven's sake! This point is essential for a *Had,* but it's important for all of us.

At almost all times I am taking a Bible study by another teacher. Many great discipleship materials are on the shelves now. I have so much to learn, and it keeps me under good, spontaneous teaching. God forbid that I would be the only teacher I would hear! If you can find a Bible study that speaks directly to some of your needs, that's all the better! I pray that you will consider maintaining a very active relationship with God through His Word for the rest of your life. We can't recognize lies if we don't know truth. Psalm 19:10–11 says of God's precepts:

> They are more precious than gold,
> > than much pure gold;
> they are sweeter than honey,
> > than honey from the comb.
> *By them is your servant warned;*
> > in keeping them there is great reward.
>
> > > > (emphasis mine)

For all of us *Hads* and former *Hads,* we need all the warnings of trouble ahead that we can get!

Thank you for allowing me to be so bold. Please don't just take my advice. Measure it against Scripture and see if these concepts line up. Show them to someone with godly wisdom you trust and see if they agree. By all means, get second opinions! I believe they are tried and true.

Isaiah 1:16–17 says, "Stop doing wrong, learn to do right!" To learn how to keep my cart from ending up in the ditches, I had to *learn* to do right! I'm *still* learning, but thank goodness my cart is staying on the path far more consistently these days. Doing right is a learned behavior that comes from being *taught*. The word *disciple* means "pupil" or "learner." We will never cease to be God's children, but when we cease learning and being teachable, we are no longer *disciples*.

"BUT BE SURE TO FEAR THE LORD AND SERVE HIM FAITHFULLY" (V.24)

The prophet Samuel's God-given prescription began with the words "Do not be afraid." As we talked through the first point, I told you that only one kind of fear was wise and that we'd come to it later. We've just arrived. *Be sure to fear the Lord.*

God is huge. He is awesome, indeed terrifying. He is powerful. He holds all the keys to life and death, ecstasy and agony. Our futures are entirely in His hands. He is sovereign, and He answers to no one. He holds the oceans in the palm of His hands. The lightning checks in with Him. But for His mercy, we would all be consumed. He is Holy and does not wink at wickedness. He lifts up and He casts down. He makes the mind and can break the mind. When He rises from His throne, His enemies scatter. He has no equal. He is complete, pure, unadulterated *otherness*.

The fear of the LORD is the beginning of
knowledge,
but fools despise wisdom and discipline.
(Prov. 1:7)

The fear of the LORD is the beginning of wisdom,
and knowledge of the Holy One is understanding. (Prov. 9:10)

Through love and faithfulness sin is atoned for;
through the fear of the LORD a man avoids evil.
(Prov. 16:6)

God hasn't forgiven you, me, or anyone else because our sins
were no big deal. He has forgiven us because of His great love.
Period. He loves us so much, He threw all our transgressions on
His own perfect Son and let Him die on a cross in our place. We
simply chose to receive the gift.

We must never take lightly all that is involved in our redemption and restoration. If we do, we will have to deal with the
Creator of the universe. I love the song "How Deep the Father's
Love for Us," written by Stuart Townend.[1] Meditate on the truths
of his words:

How deep the Father's love for us
How vast beyond all measure
That He should give His only Son
To make a wretch His treasure
How great the pain of searing loss
The Father turns His face away

As wounds which mar the Chosen One
Bring many sons to glory
Behold the man upon the cross
My sin upon His shoulders
Ashamed, I hear my mocking voice
Call out among the scoffers
It was my sin that held Him there
Until it was accomplished
His dying breath has brought me life
I know that it is finished

I will not boast in anything
No gifts, no power, no wisdom
But I will boast in Jesus Christ
His death and resurrection
Why should I gain from His reward?
I cannot give an answer
But this I know with all my heart
His wounds have paid my ransom

"CONSIDER WHAT GREAT THINGS HE HAS DONE FOR YOU" (V. 24)

Years ago I begged God in all sincerity never to let me forget what He has done for me. I could cry as easily today about the redemptive mercy applied when He last dragged me from a pit as I did at the time of my deliverance. His mercies are new every morning. God applies them to me every single day of my needy life, but I never want to lose sight of where I've been and some of the places He's had to come to my rescue.

I am convinced that the ability to remember *as if it happened yesterday* is a gift, even though some days it feels like a curse. It's worth any bad memories if I never forget God's goodness to me. I just have to remember to take any hurtful memories straight to His throne and ask Him to bathe them in His sanctifying love and grace.

I pray that He will continue to sustain an overwhelming gratitude in me and that He will do the same in you. He deserves constant gratitude, and rehearsing the great things He has done for us forms a constant protection to us. The accuser says, "Feel guilty and condemned for all the great things the Most High has had to do for you." Deliberately refuse to listen to him. The more you listen, the more he'll say. Believe God's Word instead: "There is therefore now no condemnation to them which are in Christ Jesus, who walk not after the flesh, but after the Spirit" (Rom. 8:1 KJV).

You can judge whether your consideration of the great things God has done for you flows from the Spirit—by the fruit. Healthy, Spirit-led considerations of God's great deeds release fountains of gratitude and praise from your soul. Considerations coming from the accuser poison the waters with guilt and condemnation.

> My soul glorifies the Lord
> and my spirit rejoices in God my Savior,
> for he has been mindful
> of the humble state of his servant
>
> . . . .

for the Mighty One has done great things for
    me—
holy is his name.
His mercy extends to those who fear him,
    from generation to generation. (Luke 1:46–50)

"YET IF YOU PERSIST IN DOING EVIL, BOTH YOU AND YOUR KING WILL BE SWEPT AWAY" (V. 25)

God extended complete grace and mercy to the Israelites and gave them the perfect remedy for their restoration. He tagged a vital warning to the end, however. In chapter 13 I told you about my visit to the doctor. She wrote me a prescription for an antibiotic. She also stuck a warning label on it. In a far more profound sense, that's exactly what God did with His prescription for restoration given to His confessing children. "Don't persist in doing evil."

I have no idea how being swept away could apply to us, and I don't ever want to find out. It didn't mean, either to the Israelites or to us, being swept away from His parenting. He *still* has not given up on Israel, and I believe He will completely redeem His chosen nation through their Messiah, Jesus Christ.

God has already promised that He entered into a blood covenant with us through Jesus Christ, and He will never leave us or forsake us. Being swept away could, however, apply in many other painful ways to our earthly experience. It could mean swept away from usefulness, from the fellowship of the Body of Christ, from *His fellowship* (which would be a fate I consider worse than earthly death), from our giftedness, from our places of service, or even from our earthly lives. God makes no bones about His willingness in extreme cases to take a child home if that's the only way to stop them from destruction.

Complete forgiveness and restoration is ours—even usefulness in the Body of Christ and lives of faithful service! God can work everything together for good and redeem our failures. He will gladly be strong in our weaknesses and show us His gracious favor. He can plunder the enemy and take back what Satan stole from us. But *we cannot persist in doing evil.* Just as a physician says an antibiotic will not have its full effectiveness if not taken under the prescribed conditions, God's prescription has a warning that says, "Ineffective when patient persists in doing evil." HaHa—True

God is not asking for perfection. I'm certainly no rule of thumb, but I don't mind telling you that I live a rare day without something to confess, whether the sin has been outward in word or deed or inward in attitude, motive, or omission. He did not say to the Israelites nor is He saying to us, "If you don't pull your act together and start acting perfect, you'll be swept away." He said that if they persisted in the evil that got them into their mess, they would face serious consequences. The same is undoubtedly true for us. To the woman who was caught in adultery, Christ said, "Neither do I condemn you. . . . Go now and leave your life of sin" (John 8:11).

God will empower you to obey Him with the Holy Spirit within you. Cast yourself upon Him if you don't believe you can leave a life of sin. Ask Him to raise up an army to help you and defend you against the enemy. Ask Him to do whatever He must do! You cannot persist in the evil without dire consequences.

God will enable you to obey Him! You can do all things through Christ who gives you strength (Phil. 4:13). Your feelings of hopelessness and helplessness are coming straight from the enemy. They are lies. Surrender yourself to God, withholding nothing, and ask Him to do what seems impossible. Humble yourself and receive the help He will send you as you seek it.

He who called you is faithful, and He will do it! (1 Thess. 5:24).

CHAPTER 17

A STOP
AT THE CROSS

*T*orment. That's the best word I know to describe the fiery darts of accusation impaled in the bull's-eye of the unrelieved conscience. Once we've allowed and believed God to cleanse our consciences, Satan loses the bull's-eye and can only *hope* to hit a nerve where our pasts are concerned. As long as the conscience is not clear, however, he isn't left to hope. He has a virtual certainty. His drill points straight into the nerve where it hisses unmercifully and exposes us to the agony of unrelenting shame.

What may be news to many theologically (though not experientially) is that we can sincerely confess our sin and even turn from the sin yet still die a thousand "deaths" at the stab wounds of a guilty conscience. We can quite possibly and inadvertently take God our confessions for forgiveness but not our consciences for cleansing. In so doing we leave them to the *un*mercy of the "accuser of the brethren."

A guilty conscience that *precedes* sincere repentance is the conviction of the Holy Spirit. A guilty conscience *following* sincere repentance is condemnation that is *not* coming from God. But, until we've settled the matter by faith with Him, our consciences constitute an invitational tournament for the devil.

God is the only One who can purify a conscience that has become a playground for accusation. A cleansed conscious *can* and *should* be received at the time of our repentance, but often our unrecognized unbelief blocks reception.

A guilty conscience. What could be more torturous to a believer who has walked with God and enjoyed sweet fellowship? I may not understand much William Shakespeare wrote, but these words are crystal clear:

> My conscience hath a thousand several tongues,
> And every tongue brings in a several tale,
> And every tale condemns me for a villain.[1]

Polybius wrote:

> There is no witness so dreadful, no accuser so
> terrible as the conscience that dwells in the heart
> of every man.[2]

A troubled conscience respects no one. The unredeemed can certainly still suffer from a guilty conscience, which can often be the work of the Holy Spirit to draw them to repentance and salvation. Sadly, they have no real and lasting remedy without Christ.

Obviously, the lost aren't the only ones who can deal with painful consciences. Believers who walk willingly into a season of rebellion can still bear the pangs of a guilty conscience.

If you can imagine the pain of either of the two preceding examples, can you fathom the anguish of those with *wholehearted, sincere, and pure devotion to Christ* who were seduced into a season of ungodliness? *Torment.* Until they allow God to deliver them from a guilty conscience, they are the objects of untold torture.

So often our lack of cooperation with God to finish what He started defaults us into an unknowing cooperation with the enemy of our souls. Those who remain lost will have all of eternity for torment. Satan knows that the only torment you and I will ever receive is that which he deals out to us on this earth. We do *not* have to cooperate with him. But we do have to cooperate with God if our consciences are going to be free from torment. In this chapter I hope to be able to share with you how.

I want us to study the conscience from a biblical perspective and discover how it can really—and lastingly—be cleansed. The Greek word for "conscience" in the primary biblical text I will be using in this chapter is *sundeidesis,* defined by one source as: "to be one's own witness, one's own conscience coming forward as a witness. It denotes an abiding consciousness whose nature it is to bear inner witness to one's own conduct in a moral sense. It is self-awareness. Particularly, a knowing of oneself, consciousness."[3] I hope you caught the concept of our own consciences coming forward as a witness.

The Word of God teaches us that Christ is our advocate and He pleads our case before God, the righteous Judge. Once we repent of our sins, Christ not only serves as our counselor/attorney; He also files the most glorious legal brief in the universe. He declares that all punishment and payment of fines for our crimes have been met.

You and I both know that we often still suffer from a guilty conscience even after sincere repentance, so what has gone wrong? *The Body of Christ suffers terribly from unbelief.* We often do not accept and believe the full work of God's redemption. In fact, our own consciences will go so far as to come forward as a witness—listen carefully—for the *prosecution* rather than the defense.

How I pray that we're going to learn how to allow the truth of God's Word to penetrate our hearts and minds so deeply and profoundly that our consciences will bear the exact same witness as the Holy Spirit. What a glorious event when our consciences can speak in chorus with the Spirit of God!

One of the most powerful names I've ever heard given to the conscience is "a recorder." As in *tape* recorder. That ought to make plenty of sense to any of us who know the agony of our minds rewinding and replaying an old tape incessantly. *Rewind. Play. Rewind. Play. Rewind. Play. Rewind. Play. Torment.*

We keep waiting for the tape to wear out, but it never does. Some of us are still harboring such old guilt, it's an eight-track, for crying out loud. *There is a remedy.* We'll discover that cure after we compile some vital facts offered by Scripture on the topic of conscience. The Word of God equips us with at least five facts about the conscience:

1. People with a guilty past can still enjoy a clear conscience.

Praise God! I hope you'll be blessed to know that the person God chose to say more about the conscience than anyone else in the entire Bible is the apostle Paul.

How appropriate! I don't know of a person in the entire New Testament who had more grounds for harboring guilt. By his own admission, Paul zealously persecuted Christians, seeing to their imprisonments and even to some of their deaths. He considered himself to be the least of the apostles and the chief of sinners, and yet God had completely purified his conscience—just as He can cleanse any of ours no matter how heinous the sin.

2. Good deeds cannot accomplish a clear conscience.

Referring to the veil separating the people of Israel from the Holy of Holies, Hebrews 9:9 says, "This is an illustration for the present time, indicating that the gifts and sacrifices being offered were not able to clear the conscience of the worshiper." They still can't.

We can lavishly offer gifts of talents, time, money, and make untold sacrifices, but we still won't be able to clear our own consciences. The most well-meaning *Hads* can devote themselves to a life of poverty and perpetual good works, but they still won't be able to secure a clean conscience.

Trying to earn our right to be forgiven constitutes nothing but dead works. So does attempting to make sure God never regrets forgiving and restoring us by doing all sorts of good things following our failure. More dead works. We're going to find out that all we can do to secure a clean conscience is receive the work that He's already done.

3. The Holy Spirit works with the believer's conscience.

In Romans 9:1–2, the apostle Paul said, "I speak the truth in Christ—I am not lying, my conscience confirms it in the Holy

Spirit—I have great sorrow and unceasing anguish in my heart." Paul took God at His Word, and his conscience confirmed the work of the Holy Spirit in him. While the believer's conscience and the Holy Spirit are most assuredly not synonymous, the Holy Spirit works with the conscience.

God desires that we become spiritually healthy enough through faith to have a conscience that rightly interprets the work of the Holy Spirit. A continued guilty conscience following sincere repentance can be the Holy Spirit's way of telling us that we have not allowed or believed God to complete a desired work in us.

4. The conscience is an indicator, not a transformer.

On its own, the conscience has no power to change us. In fact, without submitting to the authority and agreement of the Holy Spirit, it can often do little more than condemn and mislead us. The Spirit of God released to dwell richly through the Word of God is the only One who can completely transform a defeated life. He alone applies the abundant power not only to recognize the right thing but to do it!

5. The conscience can be seared.

This biblical fact ought to scare us half to death. You may recall the Scripture we referenced in part 1 describing those the enemy can effectively use to seduce believers in all manner of demonic doctrines. First Timothy 4:2 says, "Such teachings come through hypocritical liars, whose consciences have been seared with a hot iron."

Those willing to read books like this are likely not the ones with seared consciences, but you and I need to receive a huge "heads up" about the possibility anyway. Something is terribly wrong if we can *continue* in sin and hypocrisy without a guilty conscience. We want to have sorrow for sin! Our sorrow leading to repentance is the way the Holy Spirit bears witness that we belong to God. If you don't have it, the Spirit of God may not be dwelling in you, and you may not have salvation.

As 2 Corinthians 13:5 says, "Examine yourselves to see whether you are in the faith." If we know that we are "in the faith" but we start noticing that our conscience seems to be more callous when we sin and haven't repented, we have somehow distanced ourselves from God, and we're risking disaster. If this is you, call upon the Lord with all your might and ask Him to show you what is wrong. Seek godly counsel and the filling of the Spirit who brings sorrow that leads to repentance.

With these five facts as a foundation, let's see if we can biblically define a clean conscience before we view how to receive one. The apostle Paul offers us a wonderful definition in 2 Corinthians 1:12:

> Now this is our boast: Our conscience testifies
> that we have conducted ourselves in the world,
> and especially in our relations with you, in the
> holiness and sincerity that are from God. We have
> done so not according to worldly wisdom but
> according to God's grace.

I see two critical elements that must be present if we're going to live day to day with the joy and relief of a clean conscience: *sanctification (holiness)* and *sincerity.*

1. Pursue and practice the sincere and sanctified life in the world.

This means behaving consistently whether we're in the world or in the church. Much guilt arises in the life of the believer from practicing the chameleon life of environmental adaptation. Relief comes from finally asking God to invade the life and personality so fully that an unknown church member might observe the same person at the shopping mall or restaurant that he or she observes at church.

To offer another example, something is wrong if our co-workers would be shocked that we go to church. Most believers don't work in environments where preaching to coworkers is part of their job description, but would coworkers find our behavior inconsistent with our professed belief system at church? Consistency is a tremendous relief and a vital component in a clean conscience.

2. Pursue and practice the sincere and sanctified life in our relationships with other Christians.

Notice the apostle Paul said, "Especially in our relations with you." Oh, beloved, we've got to get *real.* We play so many games at church and in our religious life! We are caught in such a trap. Our masquerades are so important to us that we let them talk us into choosing misery over liberty. We don't get the help we need at church because so few are willing to admit they have ever had a problem.

Oh, God help us! Freedom flows like a waterfall from heaven when we surrender our lives to total authenticity before God *and* before others, particularly those at church.

Had, allow me to really speak straight to you for a moment. God will immeasurably bless your life if you are willing to get real and not act as if you've never been *Had.* In fact, He may grace your future with a greater harvest than your past if you're willing to be real.

I don't think being real necessitates telling every detail of your departure, especially if it tears down the Body of Christ rather than edifies. I do think *former Hads* should never claim to be much more than *former Hads* who have known the mercy and restoration of God. When all is said and done and you have experienced healing and consistent victory, tell what you've learned! Testify! Our churches, our neighborhoods, and our workplaces are full of *Hads* who are dying for a little hope and a way out!

I love the apostle Paul's words in 1 Corinthians 4:4: "My conscience is clear, but that doesn't make me innocent. It is the Lord who judges me." This verse states such an important part of my own personal testimony. Let me assure you, I have not been innocent. For heaven's sake, I don't remember ever getting a *chance* to be innocent! My innocence was stolen from me so early that I don't even know how it feels.

As if my victimization was not enough, I then responded wrongly, heaping sin upon sin and defeat upon defeat. No, I have not been innocent. But I can tell you this: *my conscience is clear.* I cannot write those words without wavering between wanting to cry like a baby and shout hallelujah!

Hear this testimony, *Had*. I have allowed and believed God to cleanse my conscience from all my past sins, and they were mammoth by anyone's standards. That's how I know you can have a clean conscience, too, and now let's see how.

Meditate on the transforming and freeing words of Hebrews 10:19–23:

> Therefore, brothers, since we have confidence
> to enter the Most Holy Place by the blood of Jesus,
> by a new and living way opened for us through the
> curtain, that is, his body, and since we have a great
> priest over the house of God, let us draw near to
> God with a sincere heart in full assurance of faith,
> having our hearts sprinkled to cleanse us from a
> guilty conscience and having our bodies washed
> with pure water. Let us hold unswervingly to the
> hope we profess, for he who promised is faithful.

Please notice whom the writer of Hebrews is addressing: *brothers! (And sisters!)* He is addressing believers in Christ who obviously still have need of cleansing from a guilty conscience. Praise God! I'm so glad I wasn't the only one! And, *Had,* neither are you! So, what are the biblical steps to a fresh, clean conscience?

1. Believe what God has already done for you.

The way has already been paved by the blood of Jesus. The curtain that separated man from God has been ripped from top to bottom by the tearing of the precious flesh of Jesus Christ.

2. Go into the Holy of Holies without delay, and take your heavy conscience.

In other words, approach God with every ounce of baggage weighing down your conscience. Hebrews 10:22 says, "Let us draw near." Hebrews 4:16 even tells us that because Christ has gone before us, we can leave our shame and timidity behind as we come: "Let us then approach the throne of grace with confidence, so that we may receive mercy and find grace to help us in our time of need"!

3. Approach God with absolute sincerity and repentance.

Yes!

Hebrews 10:22 says, "Let us draw near to God with a sincere heart." I'm talking about a "no-bull" approach. Spill the beans. Tell Him exactly what is bothering you and why you think your conscience is still gnawing at you. If you realize your hang-up is unbelief, confess it as sin. Take no pride with you to that altar.

If you realize you've never repented of the sin, repent with all your might. Pour out your heart before God. He is a refuge for you (Ps. 62:8). He will not reject you or forsake you. He's been waiting for you to come to Him for relief. He knows better than you do that a guilty conscience will hamstring you from pressing on to take hold of that for which Christ Jesus took hold of you (Phil. 3:12).

Get every bit of it out of your system. Play the old tape for Him (by telling Him all about what you feel and can't seem to release) and let Him hear what you keep hearing in your own mind, heart, or conscience word for word. Withhold absolutely nothing.

4. Now, ask God to cleanse your conscience just as His Word says.

Notice the words, "having our hearts sprinkled to cleanse us from a guilty conscience" (Heb. 10:22). These words can draw two different visuals from the context of the Israelites in the time of the Old Testament tabernacle.

The most obvious is the blood sprinkled by the high priest once a year on the Day of Atonement. Leviticus 16:15–16 says:

> "He shall then slaughter the goat for the sin
> offering for the people and take its blood behind
> the curtain and do with it as he did with the bull's
> blood: He shall sprinkle it on the atonement cover
> [the mercy seat, KJV] and in front of it. In this
> way he will make atonement for the Most Holy
> Place because of the uncleanness and rebellion of
> the Israelites, whatever their sins have been."

Our atonement, of course, was accomplished by the blood sacrifice of the perfect Lamb of God.

The second visual appears in a startling sprinkling of the blood in Exodus 24. The third and fourth verses say:

> When Moses went and told the people all the
> LORD's words and laws, they responded with one

voice, "Everything the LORD has said we will do."
Moses then wrote down everything the LORD had
said.

I think the more Moses wrote, the more he reconsidered
everything the Israelites just vowed they would do, and he realized they didn't have a chance of complete obedience. The next
thing we are told in Scripture is that Moses

> got up early the next morning and built an altar at
> the foot of the mountain and set up twelve stone
> pillars representing the twelve tribes of Israel. Then
> he sent young Israelite men, and they offered
> burnt offerings and sacrificed young bulls as fel-
> lowship offerings to the LORD. Moses took half of
> the blood and put it in bowls, and the other half
> he sprinkled on the altar. Then he took the Book
> of the Covenant and read it to the people. They
> responded, "We will do everything the LORD has
> said; we will obey."
>
> Moses then took the blood, sprinkled it on the
> people and said, "This is the blood of the
> covenant that the LORD has made with you in
> accordance with all these words." (Exod. 24:4–8)

Can you even imagine? The people of Israel had just
promised to obey anything God commanded them when Moses
put his hands in a bowl of blood and began to splatter them with
it. Can you picture their faces? They must have been appalled, yet

do you see the consistency of God's redemptive plan? All acceptance and approach to God is based on the blood of the sacrifice.

Theologically, I believe Moses' actions demonstrated that the blood (which foreshadowed Christ's own) was the basis of their covenant relationship with God. They were powerless to keep the letter of the law—just as we are.

You and I realize that the blood Christ shed on the cross is the means of remission for our sins. But Hebrews 10:22 says it is also the means for the complete cleansing of the consciences of those who already know Christ.

On the Day of Atonement, not only was blood sprinkled on and in front of the mercy seat; it was also sprinkled at the altar of sacrifice (described in Lev. 16:19). In fact, the high priest sprinkled the blood seven times. Seven is the number of completion or perfection in the Word of God. I believe this act foreshadowed the perfect sacrifice for sin offered centuries later when Christ gave His life on the cross.

I am asking you now to enter into a time of intense prayer and intimacy with God, telling Him how much you want to be free of your load of guilt and how desperate you are to receive a clean conscience. Ask Him to take you back to the cross (through prayer), where you first received your salvation.

This time you are not going for salvation. You are approaching the cross to have your conscience sprinkled clean. Several of the writers of both Old and New Testament Scripture talked about God taking them somewhere in "spirit." I am not implying anything mystical or unsound. I am simply suggesting that you ask God to take you in a sense in your spirit through prayer and meditation back to the cross of His precious Son. In every way, the cross was indeed the fulfillment of the altar of sacrifice.

Through prayer, ask God to take you back to the scene of Calvary and help you draw so close to Christ's cross that you can picture the blood from His wounded head sprinkling directly upon your heart.

Imagine the cross of Christ for a moment. By the time Christ gave up His life, His head would have hung forward. Victims of crucifixion ordinarily died from asphyxiation because they could no longer hold back their shoulders and hold up their heads. As Christ gave up His life for your sins and mine, the blood would have dripped from His wounded head over the thorns from His "crown."

To me the thorns are so significant because they were the sign of the curse of sin upon the earth in Genesis 3:18. When Christ wore the crown of thorns, I believe it depicted Him wearing the curse of sin upon the earth. When the blood dripped from the thorns onto the ground in front of His cross, it accomplished the perfect sprinkling of blood in front of the true altar of sacrifice.

In prayer, stand right there. Confess your wrongdoing as I have confessed mine. Tell God your need. Spiritually speaking, ask Him to allow the blood that fell from Christ's wounded head to sprinkle afresh upon your heart, mind, and soul, cleansing you from a guilty conscience. Spend time with Him there.

I don't believe a single thing is unsound about our trying to picture mentally what God has done for us spiritually. We are told to approach the throne of grace, yet it is a throne we cannot see with our eyes. I can't imagine that we're not welcome to picture it with our minds as best we can. In the same way I am helped when I allow Scripture to captivate my imagination as I approach the throne of grace, I am helped as I allow Scripture to capture my imagination as I approach the cross of Christ.

The last thing I'm suggesting is some "out of body" experience. The apostle Paul never saw the cross of Christ with his own eyes nor stood before it literally to be sprinkled by Christ's blood, yet he wrote, "May I never boast except in the cross of our Lord Jesus Christ, through which the world has been crucified to me, and I to the world" (Gal. 6:14). Can you imagine that the apostle Paul never pictured himself standing before that cross? I am convinced he did, just as I have done many times without a single hint of disapproval from God.

5. Approach God with a full assurance of faith.

Hebrews 10:22 says, "Let us draw near to God with a sincere heart in full assurance of faith, having our hearts sprinkled to cleanse us from a guilty conscience." Beloved, God is more than willing to cleanse us from the guilt of repented sin! He will *never* turn us down as we approach Him on the basis of Christ's accomplished work on Calvary.

For us to personally apply the accomplished work, however, we've got to approach Him with a full assurance of faith. In other words, we've got to believe God will do what He says He will do! Christ has already done the work, but we receive it by our faith. Christ came for the express purpose of forgiving sin and cleansing us from all unrighteousness. He wants nothing more than to give you and me the grace gift of a fresh, clean conscience with which to enjoy our full redemption, but we've got to accept it through belief! Hebrews 10:23 says, "For he who promised is faithful." You and I must hold on unswervingly to what our faithful God has promised.

Trust me on this one: Satan has gotten a lot of mileage off your guilty conscience. He's not going to want to give it up as his playground. When he comes back to accuse you, you are going to have to hold on *unswervingly* to what God has told you in His Word. The blood Christ shed upon the cross not only extended remission for your sins, it bought you a clean conscience from all repented sin. By faith you must apply and hold on tight to what the cross of Christ afforded you.

6. "Record" every bit of this process over the old tape.

Earlier in this chapter we likened the conscience to a tape recorder. We talked about how much many of us wish the old mental tape recordings would finally wear out. Sadly, countless people die with old tapes still rewinding and playing in their minds and haunting their consciences.

You see, the tape is already established in our memory. We have no way of getting rid of the tape. We make all sorts of promises like, "Today I'm just not going to think about this part of my past or my old sin a single time." We even make the commitment to God in prayer. Then by 10:00 A.M., the old mental habits kick back in and we involuntarily push rewind and play again. You see, no amount of determination or even *time* can make a powerful old tape cease playing on the recorder of our minds and consciences.

What is the answer? We have to record over the old tape with the truth of God's Word and the testimony of His fresh work! I cannot take back my past sins, but I can allow God to forgive me, to restore me, to redeem every mistake I've made, and to cleanse my guilty conscience. Thereby, through the power of the Holy Spirit, my past is reframed, and its destructive power is diffused.

When Satan comes back to taunt me, I replay the old tape with the new recording of God's forgiveness and redemption on it. I have said to the accuser, "You're right about one thing only. I did commit that sin, but God has graciously forgiven me. He has empowered me to live differently and even redeemed my mistakes. He has used my past experiences to make me compassionate and merciful. You cannot make unclean what my God has made clean. I've been to the cross and trusted Christ not only to save me from my sins but to cleanse my guilty conscience. You're too late, devil. You no longer have grounds to torment me. Your voice is strong and loud, but I refuse to believe you. I believe God, and I will hold unswervingly to the work He has accomplished in me."

What have I just demonstrated? What it sounds like when we push rewind and play on the old tape but this time with new information recorded over it. Satan hates to hear our testimonies of God's redemption so much that if you'll keep reframing it with God's truth every time the devil accuses you, he *will* stop.

Oh, beloved, let's cease cooperating with the enemy and start cooperating with our faithful God. He hates to see us in torment. How needless is an agonizing conscience when we've turned from sin! Too often we refuse to believe the cross is strong enough to cleanse our consciences! Go back to the cross where you first believed, and believe your Savior to set you free not only from your sin but from your guilt.

Let's look at one last step to a fresh, clean conscience:

7. Where possible and appropriate, make amends or restitution.

I strongly encourage you to receive sound godly counsel from someone you trust on this point. We never want to unload our guilt at the cost of someone else's unnecessary devastation. Often, however, those whom we have wronged are aware of our transgression. Sometimes we don't feel released from a past sin we've confessed and turned from because God desires for us to follow through by asking another's forgiveness or "righting a wrong."

One thing I learned without a doubt while writing *Breaking Free* is that the proud will never be free. Not ever. Humility is pivotal to liberty. Have you done everything you can to make restitution for any wrongdoing? Ask God to show you if anything, no matter how small it seems from a human perspective, is still undone.

Earlier I told you that I have not been innocent in my life but that my conscience is clean. Only over the last decade have I begun to experience twinges of "innocence" as I've come to walk with God in victory and believe the Word for my new identity. It has been indescribably wonderful! I feel more like a child in some ways than I ever felt when I was young.

The process of having my mind, soul, and heart completely cleaned out and sanctified by God has been lengthy but incomparable in my personal journey. My sins have been great, so God has required no few things of me to experience His full redemption in every area. I can assure you I have had to humble myself and ask forgiveness of a number of people. In some situations, my flesh wanted to follow up with the words, "And *you* owe *me* a huge apology! Your sin against me was worse than my sin against you!"

It's all sin, beloved. And I can tell you in retrospect that I am so glad God would not allow me to do anything less than go all the way to the line in obedience. The grace-harvest has been tremendous.

God required me to approach others expecting (and sometimes getting) nothing in return. He simply said, "Child, you go and ask forgiveness, taking full responsibility for your sin. Ask any way you might be able to make up for what you have done, then if I confirm it, *do it.*"

The more I concentrated on the log in my own eye and quit searching for the speck in others, the easier the process got. I am free today. Hallelujah! God has sovereignly ordained, however, that in my life, my own personal freedom is not enough. I want you to be free too.

Will you please? Will you do whatever it takes? Oh, beloved, it is so worth it. He is so worth it. He will grace you in ways you never dreamed possible. The work of the cross still stands! Go, beloved, and have your heart sprinkled!

> Blessed relief!
> I choose to believe
> I hold without swerving
> To what I've received

God who has promised
Is faithful to me
Blessed relief!
I choose to believe.

CHAPTER 18

GOING HOME

Dear, dear *Had,* this is where I stop and you go on without me. That's your Father's house over there. Many people can walk beside you on your road to restoration, but no one can take you that last quarter mile to your Father's arms. No person can go there but you, and you will never be healed until you do.

Oh, you might appear to others to have pulled it together. You might never fall for another seduction. You might go forward with more humility than you've ever had. You might serve with more purity of heart than you knew a mortal could have. But you will not be healed.

Before we go our separate directions, sit down with me for a few minutes on the side of this hill overlooking your Father's property. I want to tell you why. The answer is woven like a strand of golden yarn in a wayward son's robe.

You were expecting the prodigal's story, weren't you? Surely no book on Christian restoration would be complete without it. Strange that it's the most well-known, even well-loved, account of the wandering child's return to God, yet it may very well be the least personally experienced. Oh, plenty of prodigals go home, but that's not enough to heal their infected wounds.

Had, I don't want you just to read this story or even commit it to lifelong memory. I want you to leave your footprints all over its pages and live every last bit of it. Forget your familiarity with this story and forget everyone else who has ever referred to it in his testimony. You've got an appointment with God.

I'm going to share the well-known story from the less-known version of the Amplified Bible so you might not be able to anticipate each verse. Picture every word of it. Try to visualize your Father's expression when you saddle up your beast of deception, jump on its back, and leave the safety of home. Imagine the initial exhilaration of leaving your former bounds. Reflect on every single action you took outside those bounds. Then for a moment relive the spiral descent and the sickness of a growing awareness. Feel the fear. Remember the terrible pangs of insatiable hunger. Remember the depths. Then, recapture the call of your soul to go home.

This is your story, and until you let go of every other lifeline and throw yourself into it, you will remain bound, not by your seduction, but by your self-punishment.

> And He said, There was a certain man who
> had two sons;
> And the younger of them said to his father,
> Father, give me the part of the property that falls
> [to me]. And he divided the livelihood [between]
> them.
> And not many days after that, the younger son
> gathered up all that he had and journeyed into a

distant country, and there he wasted his fortune in reckless and loose-from-restraint living.

And when he had spent all he had, a mighty famine came upon that country, and he began to fall behind and be in want.

So he went and forced (glued) himself upon one of the citizens of that country, who sent him into his fields to feed hogs.

And he would gladly have fed on (and filled his belly with) the carob pods that the hogs were eating, but [they could not satisfy his hunger and] nobody gave him anything [better].

Then when he came to himself, he said, How many hired servants of my father have enough food and to spare, but I am perishing (dying) here of hunger!

I will get up and go to my father, and I will say to him, Father, I have sinned against heaven and in your sight;

I am no longer worthy to be called your son; [just] make me as one of your hired servants.

So he got up and came to his [own] father. But while he was still a long way off, his father saw him and was moved with pity and tenderness [for him], and he ran and embraced him and kissed him—fervently.

And the son said to him, Father, I have sinned against heaven and in your sight; I am no longer

worthy to be called your son—I no longer deserve
to be recognized as a son of yours!

But the father said to his bond servants, Bring
quickly the best robe—the festive, robe of
honor—and put it on him, and give him a ring
for his hand and sandals for his feet;

And bring out that [wheat-] fattened calf and
kill it, and let us revel and feast and be happy and
make merry;

Because this my son was dead, and is alive
again; he was lost and is found! And they began to
revel and feast and make merry.

But his older son was in the field, and as he
returned and came near to the house, he heard
music and dancing.

And having called one of the servant (boys) to
him, he began to ask what this meant.

And he said to him, Your brother has come,
and your father has killed that [wheat-] fattened
calf, because he has received him back safe and
well.

But [the elder brother] was angry—with deep-
seated wrath—and resolved not to go in. Then his
father came out [and] began to plead with him,

But he answered his father, Lo, these many
years I have served you, and I have never dis-
obeyed your command; yet you never gave me [so
much as] a (little) kid, that I might revel and feast
and be happy and make merry with my friends;

But when this son of yours arrived, who has
devoured your estate with immoral women, you
have killed for him that [wheat-] fattened calf!

And the father said to him, Son, you are
always with me, and all that is mine is yours.

But it was fitting to make merry, to revel and
feast and rejoice, for this brother of yours was
dead, and is alive again! He was lost and is found!

(Luke 15:11–32 AMP)

Oh, *Had,* do you remember? When you realized you had been
deceived and made a terribly foolish decision, did you try to *glue
yourself* to one of the citizens of that distant land to help you? And
they couldn't, could they? Was it a counselor or a friend who told
you nothing was wrong with you, then sent you to feed hogs?

You will find plenty that will help you stay right where you
are, but the compass in your soul is telling you that you don't
belong there. The only way out is home. A true son can stay in
the distance only so long until an overwhelming hunger that no
one can satisfy begins to gnaw at his soul.

Do you want to go home but, like the prodigal, would you
feel better about the whole thing if you just went back as a servant instead of a son? It will never work. Thousands do it, but it
never brings relief. They work maniacally trying to make up to
God for what they've done. "I am no longer worthy to be called
your son." They never were. They just never knew.

They'd feel better if they could just take a beating like a run-
away slave returned to the taskmaster. Don't you realize, *Had,*
you've already had a beating?

Oh, I see. You just want to pay some kind of penance for what you've done. Ah, still too much ego. When will we get it through our heads that our penance has already been paid? It's pretty humiliating to our pitiful egos that the only way we can come home is just to stand right there, receive, and let the Father party over us. We still want to make this thing all about us, don't we? Well, the *good news* flash is that it's not.

When you're restored, if you're truly restored, you'll be free of the most seductive yoke of all—every ounce of confidence you have ever had in your flesh.

Do you think God is going to restore you in ways that let you be proud of your hard work? *Nope.* It's not going to happen that way.

Sure, you've got a lot of work to do so that you can allow the Holy Spirit to sanctify you *through and through* and fortify you against ever riding another beast of deception off your Father's property. So did I. But restoration? God does that all by Himself. You just have to stand there as humbled as you've ever been in your life and come face-to-face with grace. When all is said and done, the only boasting you'll have left is that of a certain former murderer and relentless persecutor who enjoyed more freedom in Christ than the best of the apostles:

> May I never boast except in the cross of our
> Lord Jesus Christ, through which the world has
> been crucified to me, and I to the world. . . .
> for I bear on my body the marks of Jesus.
> (Gal. 6:14, 17)

That's all you've got left. Die to everything else.

And how about that big brother at your Father's house? He's pretty scary, isn't he? You may not realize it, but he's going to be one of the biggest obstacles Satan is going to use to keep you from returning home with your whole heart.

He may eye you. He may judge you. He may resent like crazy any hint that God may choose to use you. Oh, he is powerful. But he is not your Father, and he is not in charge.

Don't get the wrong idea. The Father loves him every bit as much as He loves you, but if big brother doesn't get that chip off his shoulder, he may find himself out in the woodshed with Dad. Oh, what he misses when he won't go to the party!

I hope never again to be a prodigal, but I surely do hope I get an invitation to many a prodigal's homecoming dance. It's pride that can't celebrate with a prodigal-come-home. Folks who won't come are still kidding themselves into thinking they did something right to be loved by their Father.

Not all big brothers are Pharisees, but I can't help reflecting one last time on that parable in Luke 18.

> To some who were confident of their own
> righteousness and looked down on everybody else,
> Jesus told this parable: "Two men went up to the
> temple to pray, one a Pharisee and the other a tax
> collector. The Pharisee stood up and prayed about
> himself: 'God, I thank you that I am not like other
> men—robbers, evildoers, adulterers—or even like
> this tax collector. I fast twice a week and give a
> tenth of all I get.'

"But the tax collector stood at a distance. He
would not even look up to heaven, but beat his
breast and said, 'God have mercy on me, a sinner.'

"I tell you that this man, rather than the other,
went home justified before God. For everyone
who exalts himself will be humbled, and he who
humbles himself will be exalted." (Luke 18:9–17)

Justified. That's a huge word. If the truth be known, we don't
really like God's rules. They minimize our egos. And until we are
crucified, we are nothing but a bunch of walking egos.

We desperately want to have something to do with our justification. We spend untold energies trying to justify ourselves. Oh,
what freedom to give up! Plunder your disaster until you find the
crown jewel of unjustifiable justification!

Big brother won't mind if you come back as long as you hang
your head and wear your shame. But when God has the audacity
to give you a little dignity back and you dare lift your radiant face
to heaven in liberated praise, big brother may be appalled!

And we know that in all things God works
for the good of those who love him, who have
been called according to his purpose. For those
God foreknew he also predestined to be conformed to the likeness of his Son, that he might
be the firstborn among many brothers. And
those he predestined, he also called; those he
called, he also justified; those he justified, he also
glorified.

What, then, shall we say in response to this? If
God is for us, who can be against us? He who did
not spare his own Son, but gave him up for us
all—how will he not also, along with him, graciously give us all things? Who will bring any
charge against those whom God has chosen? It is
God who justifies. Who is he that condemns?
Christ Jesus, who died—more than that, who was
raised to life—is at the right hand of God and is
also interceding for us. (Rom. 8:28–34)

God may use men to guide the prodigal home, to teach the
prodigal how to stay in his own yard, and even help discipline the
prodigal, . . . but it is *God who justifies.* He does it by applying the
ransom of your *biggest* Brother's death to your account.

Had, you don't ever have to apologize that God has forgiven
you and has loved you enough to accept you without question
and restore you. If you surrender all you've been through to His
purposes, you don't have to apologize if He uses your disaster for
your good. You don't even have to apologize if He dares to use
you shamelessly "after what you have done."

If you really learned your lesson, you're not likely ever to be
anything but profoundly humbled again, but humility before
God and others doesn't mean apologizing for God's embarrassing
shows of affection to you.

Face it! God's love for us is scandalous! I look at the words of
Philippians 2:7. They say that Christ "made himself of no reputation" (KJV), and I think, *That Christ would dare use someone like
me proves that He didn't care much about His reputation!*

What is God asking of us? Unabashed, unhindered, completely abandoned *repentance!* No faking. No hedging. No blaming. No excuses. Just, "Have mercy on me, a sinner!" That's what He wants out of all of us!

Dietrich Bonhoeffer wrote:

> He who is alone with his sins is utterly alone. It may be that Christians, not withstanding corporate worship, common prayer, and all their fellowship in service, may still be left to their loneliness. The final breakthrough to fellowship does not occur because, though they have fellowship with one another as believers and as devout people, they do not have fellowship as the undevout, as sinners. The pious fellowship permits no one to be a sinner. So everyone must conceal his sin from himself and from their fellowship. Many Christians are unthinkably horrified when a real sinner is suddenly discovered among the righteous. So we remain alone with our sin, living in lies and hypocrisy. The fact is we are sinners![1]

Brennan Manning, in one of the most remarkable books I have ever read, follows Bonhoeffer's quote with his own words:

> At Sunday worship, as in every dimension of our existence, many of us pretend to believe we are sinners. Consequently, all we can do is pretend to believe we have been forgiven. As a result, our

whole spiritual life is pseudo-repentance and pseudo-bliss.

The spiritual future of ragamuffins consists not in disavowing that we are sinners but in accepting that truth with growing clarity, rejoicing in God's incredible longing to rescue us in spite of everything.[2]

Manning asks a very disturbing question and one that all of us are more than wise to try to answer:

Biblically, there is nothing more detestable than a self-righteous disciple. He is so swollen with conceit that his mere presence is unbearable. However, a nagging question arises. Have I so insulated myself in a fortified city of rationalizations that I cannot see that I may not be as different from the self-righteous as I would like to think?[3]

Thankfully, God even has mercy on the self-righteous Pharisee who repents. After all God has done for me, to withhold the Pharisee the right to splash in the river of forgiveness would make me a bigger one than he. If we have come to this point in our journey and we still have a shred of self-righteousness left, we are still kidding ourselves about our sin. We are still a great distance from home. To the glory of God, we can still get there, but not without stopping in the valley of repentance and stooping to observe our own reflection in the pond.

I want to tell you a story. A true story. I watched it second-hand and with my very own eyes. It happened in the family of someone I've known for years. I don't even know if they "got it." But I got it. And this is my rendition of it.

Once upon a time there was an unhappy couple. She said it was because they were so mismatched. She married beneath herself. In actuality, they were not altogether different. After all, the reality is that baggage attracts baggage. One set may have looked more like a brown paper sack and the other like fine, leather Gucci, but it's all baggage.

She kept a cold heart toward him because she knew he had to be bad. Somewhere deep inside of her it was the very thing that had first attracted her, but she would never admit to such a thing. Yes, she knew he had to be bad. And just as she suspected, he was. His sins were many and grievous—by anyone's standards. Terrible and as broad in consequence as a thundering black horizon. She caught him in his sin, and shame reverberated throughout the broken family.

He fell on his knees in repentance and begged God to save his life and spare his family. He did. Though the change in the man was obvious, some things never changed. She held on to her cold heart and wore her unforgiveness like a corsage of dead roses. It was her badge of honor to remind her children she would never forgive. She said it was for their sake.

He took his punishment for years, as did the children. If she had only known that the effects of her coldness, self-righteousness, and perpetual punishment were just as destructive to their trembling home as were his terrible sins.

One day she died. The chains of bondage draped a body that had finally turned as cold as her heart. The last remaining blackened petals on her corsage of dead roses fell to the floor. She died in her bitterness.

He grieved for awhile and strangely would have had her back—if he could have.

Then God did a most peculiar thing. In the man's aging years—years spent feeding hungry people and ministering to any who would have him—God brought him another mate. One whose heart was warm with affection. God blessed the latter years of the old man's life with joy and usefulness—yes, even after grievous sins.

His wife of many years never committed any such sins, yet she drowned in the gall of her own self-righteousness—proud to the very last breath that she had never sinned against her family like he.

And he? Well. He lived happily ever after.

Peculiar, isn't it?

Had, all God wants out of you and me when we come home is repentance and humility. Those two things are so foreign to our human, self-deprecating *little-man syndrome* that God thinks they're worth celebrating every time He sees them. Frankly, they make God want to party.

Do you remember the part of the prodigal parable when music and dancing echoed all over the countryside? I have always found the terminology of David intriguing when he cried out in repentance after his heinous sins, "Make me to hear joy and gladness; that the bones which thou hast broken may rejoice" (Ps. 51:8 KJV).

David had been a true lover of God. He had known glorious intimacy with a heavenly Father whose glory he had seen and words he had heard. He was the very one who penned the words, "Know that the LORD has set apart the godly for himself; / the LORD will hear when I call to him" (Ps. 4:3). But he may not have known way back then that the Lord also hears when the ungodly call to him.

In Psalm 51, David was a man stricken by the grief of his own sin. A godly man who turned from the path and foolishly did ungodly things. He was seduced not by a woman but by a powerful unseen force. He denied responsibility for his sins and rationalized his behavior for as long as he could. Then he broke. Leave it to David not to be satisfied with a partial restoration.

David had known the sacred romance. I believe he would rather have died than to be forgiven but held at arm's distance from a God of no more chances.

"Make me to hear joy and gladness; that the bones which thou hast broken may rejoice." Whose joy and gladness did

David want to hear? Oh, beloved, without a doubt I believe it was God's! His Father's! "Abba, my Abba! I can only bear to come home if You are glad to see me! If I could only hear Your joy over my return, these bones that You have broken will rejoice!"

David couldn't have stood it any other way. Line it up beside Jesus' parable of the prodigal, and you find a perfect example why David was a man after God's own heart. If he couldn't return to God's heart, he couldn't bear to return to God's home.

Had, you will never be healed any other way. Do not go back to your Father's table to eat the crumbs on the floor like a dog. Think more of His redemption than that. Do not go back to your Father's house just to be safe. He wants far more for you than that. You will never heal if you only go back to your Father's *home*. You must go back to His *heart*. Closer than you've ever been.

Ah, there He is just now. Coming across the field. He is running in your direction. He doesn't even see me right now. He only has eyes for you. Forget your speeches. He wants to hug you. He wants to kiss you. Your healing will come in your very own Abba's tight and passionate embrace. Let Him hold you so close that you can hear His heart pounding from having run to you.

Don't stop Him when He wants to put a robe on your back. A ring on your finger. And sandals on your feet. Do not take this moment from Him. Feast on the fatted calf. Then listen as He makes you to hear *His* joy and gladness. Press your ear to the floor and let your heart be caught in the rhythm of the steps of your Father's dance. Then get up off of that floor and let your broken bones rejoice. That will forever be the most authentic sign of a prodigal's gratitude.

Don't be afraid! He wouldn't run like that if He weren't glad to see you! Look at the way He's springing up that hill! He's yelling something. I can't quite make it out. Oh, now I hear it. He's yelling, "Son!"

That was your name all along! Not *Good* or *Proud*.

"Son!"

Farewell, *Had.*

Do not gloat over me, my enemy!
Though I have fallen, I will rise,
Though I sit in darkness,
    the LORD will be my light.
(Micah 7:8)

I tricked you into thinking
I would never be all right.
That's what I thought too.
I lied.
My God thought differently
And I've decided to believe Him
Instead of you.
My enemy,
You've been *Had*.

ENDNOTES

Chapter 1

1. Spiro Zodhiates et al., eds., *The Complete Word Study Dictionary: New Testament Word Study Series* (Chattanooga, Tenn.: AMG Publishers, 1991), #794, 281.

2. Charles Spurgeon, *Spurgeon on Prayer and Spiritual Warfare* (Pittsburgh, Pa.: Whitaker House, 1998), 512.

Chapter 2

1. Beth Moore, *Praying God's Word: Breaking Free from Spiritual Strongholds* (Nashville: Broadman & Holman Publishers, 2000), 276–77.

2. Brennan Manning, *Ruthless Trust: The Ragamuffin's Path to God* (San Francisco: HarperSanFrancisco, 2000), 117–18.

3. "A Lust for Profit," *Online U.S. News,* March 2000.

4. Steve Gallagher, "Devastated by Internet Porn," Pure Life Ministries, 15 December 2000, www.purelifeministries.org/mensarticle1.htm.

5. Ibid.

Chapter 3

1. Zodhiates, ed., *The Complete Word Study Dictionary: New Testament,* #4301, 1222.

2. Charles Ryrie, *Basic Theology: A Popular Systematic Guide to Understanding Biblical Truth* (Chicago: Moody Press, 1999), 168.

Chapter 4

1. Spiro Zodhiates, ed., "Old Testament Lexical Aids," *The Hebrew-Greek Key Study Bible* (Chattanooga, Tenn.: AMG Publishers, 1990), 1556.
2. Ibid., #8706, 1556.
3. Brennan Manning, *The Ragamuffin Gospel* (Sisters, Ore.: Multnomah Publishing, 2000), 31–32.
4. Manning, *Ruthless Trust*, 13.

Chapter 5

1. *Practical Word Studies in the New Testament,* vol. 2 (Chattanooga, Tenn.: Leadership Ministries Worldwide, 2001), 1801.
2. James Strong, *The New Strong's Concise Dictionary of Bible Words* (Nashville: Nelson Reference, 2000), 56.
3. Zodhiates, ed., *The Complete Word Study Dictionary: New Testament,* 954.

Chapter 7

1. Darlene Zschech, "Shout to the Lord," © 1993, Darlene Zschech/Hillsong Publishing (adm. in the U.S. and Canada by Integrity's Hosanna! Music)/ASCAP, c/o Integrity Music, Inc., 1000 Cody Road, Mobile, AL 36695. Used by permission.
2. Zodhiates, ed., "The New Testament Lexical Aids," *Key Study Bible*, #6038, 1688–89.

Chapter 9

1. Spurgeon, *Spurgeon on Prayer and Spiritual Warfare,* 502.
2. Zodhiates, ed., "New Testament Lexical Aids," *Key Study Bible,* #1921, 1621.

Chapter 10

1. *Merriam Webster's Collegiate Dictionary,* 10th ed. (Springfield, Mass.: Merriam-Webster, Inc., 1997), 730.

Chapter 11

1. Spurgeon, *Spurgeon on Prayer and Spiritual Warfare,* 501.

Chapter 15

1. Edward Mote, "The Solid Rock," public domain.

Chapter 16

1. Stuart Townend, "How Deep the Father's Love for Us," Copyright © 1995 Kingsway's Thank you Music/PRS/All rights in the Western hemisphere administered by EMI Christian Music Publishing. Used by permission.

Chapter 17

1. John Bartlett, ed. Justin Kaplan, *Bartlett's Familiar Quotations: A Collection of Passages, Phrases, and Proverbs Traced to Their Sources in Ancient and Modern Literature,* 16th ed. (New York: Little Brown & Co., 1992), #15, 166.
2. Ibid., #11, 85.

3. Zodhiates, ed., *The Complete Word Study Dictionary: New Testament*, #4893, 1339.

Chapter 18

1. Dietrich Bonhoeffer, cited in Manning, *The Ragamuffin Gospel*, 131–32.
2. Manning, *The Ragamuffin Gospel*, 132.
3. Ibid., 133.

Notes

4-20-08   Called DH to tell him no longer double-life in spite of my double spouse. Bad response. Feeling good today

4-29-08   Gave everything back, to him. Cut off all lines of every tie. Feel a sense of freedom like never before!

5-1-08   In the beginning stages of intimacy with my true Savior.